The story you are about to read is based on a
series of actual events.

Some names have been changed at the request of
those involved.

*"The woods are lovely, dark and deep.
But I have promises to keep,
And miles to go before I sleep…"*

Robert Frost

ALEX SANDERS 1986

A VOICE IN THE FOREST,
Conversations with Alex Sanders

Copyright 1999 by Trident Publications
All rights reserved. No part of this book may be used or reproduced in any manner whatsoever without written permission from Trident Publications, except in the case of brief quotations embodied in critical articles or reviews. All artwork is copyrighted and the rights remain with the artist.

Special First Edition Printing, October 1999

Preface by Morven
Cover art by David Taylar Daniels
Photographs of Alex Sanders courtesy of
National Archive of Lesbian and Gay History,
Richard C. Wandel Collection

Trident Publications
P.O. Box 990591, Boston, MA 02199

A VOICE IN THE FOREST

Conversations with

Alex Sanders

A True Story

By Jimahl

TRIDENT
PUBLICATIONS

ACKNOWLEDGMENTS

This book could never have been completed without the limitless encouragement of the following people:

David, my partner of many years, who didn't run away screaming every time someone showed up on the doorstep with a Spirit Board.

Morven, my teacher and Witch Queen, who is always ready with a word of encouragement when I need it most.

Paul, Phoenix, Asha, and Finbar – for your unwavering faith in the finished project.

And to everyone involved in these remarkable events - this is not only a story about Alex – It is also a story about each of us.

CONTENTS

Preface by Morven	9
Introduction	13
A Voice in the Forest	16
Necromancy	43
The Second Group Session	67
Dreams and Questions	90
Descent into Winter	100
A Light in the Forest	108
Asha and Finbar Meet Alex	119
Promises to Keep	133
Asha and Jimahl Contact Alex	150
Dark Water	160
The Final Communication	169
The Green That Keeps on Growing	174
Afterthoughts	182

Epilogue	192
About the Author	195
About Morven (Preface)	196
About the Artist	198
About Trident Publications	199

PHOTOGRAPHS

Alex Sanders, 1986	3
Hail and Farewell	191

PREFACE

by Morven

If I were you, I'd be doing the same thing you're doing: reading the Preface to try to find out who this guy Jimahl is and what makes him think he really contacted Alex Sanders. After all, who the heck is Jimahl anyway? You've never run into him at festivals, he doesn't post to alt.pagan, and he hasn't appeared on talk radio or Halloween interviews.

Jimahl joined my coven as a new student, though one with an impressive grasp of the Craft and a little experience in Ceremonial magick. It was April 1988 and, as it turned out, less than two weeks before Alex Sanders passed through the veil. Since then, Jimahl has completed his training and trained his own students, all the while doing what I - and every teacher- both fears and desires: surpassing his teacher. His rituals are full of poetry, beauty, and power, his insight on dreams and magickal mysteries — priceless. And if that weren't enough, he is a warm and witty person and one of my most trusted and dearest friends in the Craft.

He is also something quite rare these days — a "natural" psychic and seer. So, it was no surprise to me that he would "get someone" while using the spirit board one summer night while camping. And, strangely, it was simultaneously not surprising and the most incredible thing on earth to realize he was "getting" *Alex*.

Alex Sanders, a controversial figure whose exploits were often exposed in the English tabloids, was chronicled in 1969 in *King of the Witches* by June Johns and approximately two years later in *What Witches Do* by Stewart Farrar. A natural magician with a flair for publicity and the dramatic, Alex was both reviled and praised for bringing Witchcraft to the general public. His goal was to make it more accessible, which he certainly did, but detractors were horrified by his pandering to the press and his giving away of the Craft secrets.

When I met Alex in March of 1987, he was an older, calmer man, even frail. Gone was the arrogant showman of the late 60s and early 70s. He was pleasant, good-natured, and most sincere in his love of the Goddess and his hopes for the future of the Craft. It was that aspect of his personality that came through during the sessions described in this book.

I am not sure how much of the Alex Sanders legend is true, and how much might be attributed to Alex's exaggerations — Johns' book has some rather wild tales in it, as does Farrar's. But this I know: the communications Jimahl describes here happened. He has changed some of the names and physical descriptions of people and places to protect privacy, but these sessions *did* occur. And it is my strong belief that he contacted Alex, or at least some astounding entity capable of reading all our minds to find out not only what we were thinking of — and a few things we never even thought of — but all we knew of Alex. Then this incredible entity consistently imitated him, at our whim. Pretty hard work when the entity could have easily just told us he was a Being of Light from Mars or something.

If you're not an Alexandrian (that is, a follower of the particular tradition of Witchcraft that Alex Sanders founded), you may wonder why these sessions are so important. The obvious answer would be that Alex has an important message about the Goddess. Beyond that, there is something equally important. In this day of sheer materialism, these sessions are profound because they are direct contact with the unknown, with that which has gone before, with the world beyond MTV, email, mass consumerism, and the evening news. This chronicle is something you can read, the whole while repeating to yourself:

>It's *NOT* only a movie…

Because this is real. This is *not* just special effects.

Blessed Be,
Morven
August 29, 1999

INTRODUCTION

Alex Sanders, known in his lifetime as "King of the Witches" and the founder of the Alexandrian tradition of Wicca, died in 1988.

Alex, along with Gerald Gardner, remains one of the most imposing influences responsible for the resurgence of Wicca, or the Craft of the Wise, within the Twentieth Century.

He seemed determined from an early age to learn the Ancient Art of Witchcraft. His unique approach to Wicca, coupled with his tireless devotion to the Old Gods, created a new wave of interest in the Craft. It is a wave still cresting today as generations of new students step foot into a Magick Circle for the first time.

There were undoubtedly many covens operating at the time of his death that traced their lineage directly back to Alex. I was a member of one of these covens, Na Fineachan Glice (NFG) located in Eastern Massachusetts.

When Alex first passed away in 1988, his spirit seemed extremely accessible during ritual. Many Alexandrians described a sense of him present in their celebrations. This sensation seemed especially acute during initiation rituals when often the blindfolded postulate, poised on the brink of the ritual circle for the first time, would describe being embraced or kissed by "someone" just before entering the consecrated space.

For a long while after his death, this acute awareness of Alex persisted, perhaps associated directly with our sense of loss. The wounds of his passing eventually healed. Time pressed on, each new season bringing another. Years went by. The family of NFG continued to grow and expand. To date, five new covens have been born of NFG and continue to thrive in the New England area.

Then, in one strange night, everything changed.

At Lammas in 1998, while camping in the forest of New Hampshire, a handful of NFG Elders made a startling discovery. We were attempting to use a Spirit Board around the campfire one evening. In the illumination of the leaping fire, we decided to try to contact the spirit of Alex Sanders. To our surprise, a spirit readily established a strong connection with us and convincingly identified himself as Alex Sanders.

Over a period of many months, the communication with Alex continued. The book you now hold in your hands is the result of our mutual efforts to document this remarkable story and to preserve Alex's messages. It is my hope that the spirit of Alex Sanders will touch your life as deeply as he has ours.

May the Gods Preserve the Craft,
Jimahl
Lammas 1999

Chapter One

A Voice in the Forest

It is dark in the woods of New Hampshire, especially when the moon is barely past New. It is late on a July night in 1998. There are six of us camping together. Our tent sites, sheltered by evergreen and hardwood, are spaced randomly around the edges of a large field. In the daylight the spaces we inhabit are clearly visible from the field, but in the shadows it becomes difficult to find my way through the trees. I fumble at the edge of the woods, where I imagine I see a path. The sound of laughter drifts through the tangled shrubbery. It is enough of a lead for me to follow and a few moments later I make my way into the campsite carrying an armload of firewood. Phoenix is kneeling in the fire ring, arranging a sizable stack of twigs into a pyramid.

"I'm going to build a fire," he declares with a smile. I understand his excitement. We are from the city and this is an adventure to us. He accepts my humble offering of combustible substance and goes back to his project. "It'll be my first fire," he says confidently.

"Well, make it a good one," I respond, "It's getting pretty damn cold out here tonight."

There is a picnic table next to the fire pit and Morven is seated there. She is lighting candles from a box of candle stubs, one by one, and placing them in the neck of empty bottles. They illuminate the table clumsily and the effect of the shifting light in the trees above us is eerie. Morven is my teacher. I have studied the Craft with her for over a decade.

Even now, responsible for a coven of my own, she remains my closest friend in matters of the occult.

I sit across from her and assist with the candles. "Very elegant," I joke and she smiles.

There is a sense of timelessness to Morven. I remember how she looked earlier in the day.

I found her walking in the woods wearing a ritual robe and shawl. Except for her conventional eyeglasses, she looked as if she had stepped out of a fairy tale.

"Have you seen Raven and Jack?", she asks quietly. But before I can answer there is the familiar sound of humans making yet another path through the dark undergrowth and the couple emerge from the shadows into the campsite. Jack carries more wood and Phoenix accepts it gratefully.

"Make sure you get a lot of twigs and small stuff going first," Jack advises. I know he is familiar with building a fire as I have spent many an evening lounging in front of the fireplace of the old farmhouse he shares with Raven.

"The lake is beautiful tonight," Raven says, taking a seat next to Morven at the picnic table. "And the stars…" She sighs and pulls her wool cloak close around her. Of all of us, she is the only one who brought something warm to wear. It's obvious she's a pro at camping. She thinks of everything.

"It's July – almost August for that matter. Why is it so cold?" I wasn't really complaining, just saying out loud what every one else was thinking.

"The cold keeps the mosquitoes away," Jack says matter-of-factly. He comes over to the table and sits down next to his wife. Jack is as tall and slender as a sapling. Raven leans into his embrace.

"It'll be better when Phoenix gets the fire going," Morven says loud enough for Phoenix to hear. And true to his promise, the first sputter of fire is heard behind us. The smell of the smoke drifts to us like incense – and fills our heads with the sound of the forest around us.

"Now wait until the fire catches hold," Jack coaches, "Then add some of the smaller logs". Phoenix is dancing around the fire pit like a conjurer – the glow of the fire illuminates his muscular body. He begins to recite aloud a centuries-old invocation to the elemental spirits. I watch him happily. He is my student, and it is exciting to see him revel in such a primordial setting.

"He's done it," I call out and Phoenix beams back at me from beyond the brave new tower of flame. "Congratulations!"

The trail of fire twists and turns upward, transforming the campsite in a few magic moments into a ring of golden light.

Paul emerges sleepily from the tent where he has been resting. He rubs his eyes, as if the campfire was the first light of morning.

"What's all the shouting about?" he asks and before an answer can be offered, asks, "Anything left to eat? I'm hungry."

Paul joins Phoenix for a moment at the fireside. I watch the two of them laughing at the roar of the fire.

Morven takes her cue from Paul and retires briefly into the extra tent where our communal food is stored. She returns with two paper shopping bags overflowing with junk food. Cookies, potato chips, pretzels, cheese, crackers all spill out onto the picnic table.

Jack produces, as if by magic, a bottle of wine from the shadows. The cork gets out of the way easily and the wine is poured into paper cups. I sit at the table and watch my friends by candlelight. I think how complete my life seems at this moment. The sound of their laughter, the ruddy complexion of their faces, and the fine crackling of the campfire become images that I consciously try to burn into my memory.

Remember this when you're back at the office, I remind myself, *remember the earth beneath your bare feet and the smell of the burning wood.*

I don't remember who suggested it first. But at this point it was suggested that we play with the hand-made Spirit Board that Paul had packed. I had joked with him as we struggled to get all of our gear into manageable portions. Paul was known for over-packing. "What self-respecting witch is going camping without their Spirit Board?" he argued.

The familiar box was retrieved from his tent and set up on the picnic table. We had to move the junk food to the side to make room for the board. "Who's up first?" I ask, meaning, of course, who would work the planchette. I guess I was misunderstood to be a volunteer. Paul sat down opposite me and said something like "I'll give it a try with you."

Morven found a damp notebook and a pen that had been used earlier in the day to draft a grocery list and agreed to take notes. This proved to be a good decision as Morven is able to make fast and accurate notes. She sat down closest to the campfire for visibility reasons, which just happened to be the farthest away from the Spirit Board. The others placed themselves between Morven and the board and we waited patiently for something to happen.

We didn't have a long wait, as a response to our question "Is anybody there?" came rapidly. The planchette stirred with an audible groan and moved across the board. It was actually creaking like a rusty hinge as it moved.

The following documentation of our first session with the Spirit Board is adapted largely from Morven's meticulous notes. I have edited out the inevitable nonsense as the planchette began to move. I have also eliminated or altered information received which was intended for specific individuals, but considered too personal to share publicly.

As Morven later recalled: "When I could remember who said what, I've noted it. However, the planchette moved so fast that evening, I barely had time to transcribe. I think Jimahl was asking most of the questions during this session."

"Is anybody there?" I ask cautiously.

YES

"Who is this?" I continue. Paul is looking at me as if to say "I'm not moving it, *are you?*" I return an equally puzzled expression and watch the planchette spell out:

Q U E S T I O N   M E

"Are you telling us to ask a question?"

YES

"Tell us who you are."

The planchette continues to move in that awkward way – it seems as if we are communicating with a very old spirit. There is a series of nonsensical responses. I get impatient and threaten to dismiss the spirit.

"We're going to let you go if you don't start making sense," I say aloud.

NO

"Are you a spirit?" someone asks.

JIN

"Are you telling us you're a Djinn?" Morven asks.

YES

"You're a fire elemental king?" I pose a clumsy question as I try to remember what I had read about the structure of the Elemental Kingdoms.

NO

"You're a fire elemental though?"

YES

"Have you come to us because of the fire Phoenix built?"

YES

"Tell us about fire elementals."

YOU SEE ME

"Where – in the fire?"

YES

"Are you a genii?"

YES

"What other elementals are here?"

EARTH

"Is there anything you can share with us as witches?"

WE COME WHEN WE R CALLD

"We have the ability to summon?"

YES

"That's because we are witches?"

BELIEVE

"Because we believe?"

YES

We speak for a few more minutes with the Djinn and then Phoenix and Raven are anxious to try the planchette. Paul and I relinquish our positions gladly.

Unfortunately, the planchette doesn't move at all for the two of them and after a few frustrated attempts, Raven asks if Jack will give it a try with her. It seems logical that the two of them would have good results.

Raven asks most of the questions this time around.

"Is someone here?"

YES

"Were you there just a minute ago and not answering?"

NO

"What is your name?"

A T I C

"Do you mean an attic like in a house?"

A T I C   YES

"Are you from *our* attic?"

YES

"What are you?"

D E D

"Are you a spirit of a dead person?"

YES

"Did you come camping with us?"

YES

"Did you see me take the camping stuff out of the attic?"

YES

"When you were alive, did you live in our house?"

YES

"Tell us who you are."

To the mutual surprise of Raven and Jack, the entity proceeds to spell out the name of a former resident of their old house – a ghost that has been seen in their home several times. They laugh nervously and the session ends abruptly.

The idea that their household ghost decided to go camping with Raven and Jack seems funny and we all have a good laugh about it. We continue our entertainment for a while longer with minimal results, trying many variations on the partnering. Then someone suggests that Paul and myself take a turn again.

Morven would later write:

"Paul and Jimahl were on the planchette again. I was transcribing. Paul and Jimahl decide they want to try to contact Alex Sanders. We all agreed they give it a try since they seem to make a good team. Where I could remember who said what, I've noted it. However, the planchette moved so fast that evening I barely had time to transcribe, so I couldn't always note who said what. I could, however, remember what I said, so you'll see my name a lot. I think that Jimahl was asking most of the questions in this session. An interesting note: In the first group of sessions, the planchette creaked. During this session, the planchette did *not* creak, this was unusual."

"We would like to contact Alex and only Alex. Is Alex Sanders available to communicate with us?"

YES

"Alex, is this you?"

5 K I S

Morven recognizes the abbreviation for the five-fold kiss – a traditional Wiccan greeting. "Alex, you give us the 5-fold Kiss?"

YES

"Alex, is this really you?"

YES

"You haven't reincarnated yet?"

NO

"Why are you staying on the astral?"

2000

"You're staying until the year 2000?"

YES

"Is that okay with you?"

YES

"Alex, do you remember Lady Morven?"

YES

"Any special message for her?"

TEACH THEM TO LOVE GODESS

At this point, we are all staring at each other like deer caught in the headlights. My fingertips are trembling lightly on the planchette next to Paul's hands. There is a tremendous amount of excitement in the air and it is difficult to concentrate on keeping the connection. I seem to remember a pause here where everyone takes a deep breath. I then decide to present the entity with a qualifying test to make sure this is indeed Alex.

"Alex, do you mind being tested?"

NO

Since Morven was the only one present who had actually met Alex, I asked her to devise a test for him. Morven would later write:

"I was thinking about the last time I saw Alex. He was sitting in a large stuffed chair, facing me, smiling, with a glass of white wine in his right hand. I thought to myself: *Alex, all you have to do is say 'white' or 'wine' – either one – it's not hard*. I write the words 'white wine' on the top right corner of the paper on which I am taking notes. I remember that I tap Jack, who is on my right, on the arm and point to the words. He nods. No one to my left – Jimahl or Paul – can see this because it's extremely dark (new moon) and there are boxes of crackers and snacks between the notebook and them. No one notices that Jack looks at the notebook and nods."

Jimahl remembers:

"I was very anxious at this point to find out if this was really Alex. My head was filled with images of him. I had a very strange feeling that we were really onto something that would reshape all of our lives in ways we could not possibly comprehend. *Come on, Alex,* I thought, s*ay something….* I had no idea of what sort of test Morven had devised. No one was saying anything. The moment seemed to hang there forever and then the planchette started to move again."

W I N E

"Wine!" Paul calls out. He spelled the word "wine".

Morven shows us the words on her notebook and speaks them aloud, as it is so dark we have trouble reading her notes when they are in front of our eyes. The campfire has sunken down into embers and there is only the candlelight from two tapers and a couple of citronella buckets.

There is a short pause in the process while people gasp in awe. Morven would later note:

"Jimahl and Paul admirably keep their hands on the planchette and maintain their composure. I am concurrently in complete shock that this happened and yet at the same time feel that this is absolutely normal and why should I be surprised... I mutter a silent thank you to Alex and suggest we continue."

"Alex, is this really you?" I am remembering Alex's death in 1988. I was a new student of the Craft at the time. I calculate quickly. *He's been dead for ten years*, I think to myself, *ten years*!

YES

"You've been there all along?"

YES

I ask if anyone has any questions. Morven suggests one.

"Who is Azarak?"

H O R N E D 1

Morven suggests another question.

"Who is Zomelak?" (Note: Azarak and Zomelak are two archaic names used in the traditional Witches

Rune. There seems to be an ongoing academic debate as to the origin of them)

S U N G O D

"Azarak and Zomelak are God names?"

YES

"Alex, are you happy with us?"

YES

"What can you tell us about our coven family?"

G R O W

"Are you with us when we cast a circle?"

M O S T

"You're with us most of the time?"

YES

"Who initiated you?" This question came from Morven.

R A I S E D 1 F R E D

"Is Fred someone's mundane name?"

YES

"Can you tell us about magick?"

W O R S H I P

"Magic is worship?"

G O D S

"Worship the Gods and Goddesses?"

YES

The questions were coming from the group as quickly as Alex's responses now. Someone asked:

"What is it like after you die?"

D R E A M

"You mean it's surreal?" Raven asked.

YES

"Was your work finished when you passed?"

R E A D Y

"Did you leave anything unfinished?"

YES

"What?"

GIFT

"A gift you meant to give?"

YES

"Who was the gift for?"

STUDENTS

"Which students?"

ALL

"What was the gift?"

BOOKS

"You mean you had other books?"

YES

"Were they already written when you died?"

U KNOW

"You're saying we know about these books?"

YES

"Is there anything else you want to share?"

HI LUV

"Are you talking to Morven?"

YES

Morven later remarked that Alex used to say, "Hi, luv" to people, including her when she met him.

"Do you have a message for each of us?"

YES

For the next quarter hour or so, Alex proceeded to deliver a series of personal messages to each of us who were present, and many people not present who were part of our extended Wiccan family. Each of the messages was concise, almost cryptic. Some consisted of a mantra-like sentence with one or two words. But when delivered to those for whom they were intended, the messages had a profound effect. In many cases, Alex seemed to be addressing a particular need that the individual had which had never been articulated to anyone else.

For example, to someone who had stopped formally practicing the Craft over a decade ago, Alex said simply:

COME BACK

What surprised Morven was not only the appropriateness of each message, but in many cases, the typical witty Alex sense of humor. To one of our group who is an eternal optimist, Alex said:

MAGIC IS GREAT

We laughed because we could actually hear the person saying that. Alex had picked up on this person's personality. And, finally, to someone who had been very outwardly anxious recently, Alex said:

CALM DOWN

In the months to come, many of the messages that were received from Alex began to unfold in a prophetic way within the context of our individual lives. We found ourselves reflecting again and again on his words – finding new meaning in them each time – like a complex and rare flower with petals removed only to reveal another layer of petals.

When Alex had nearly exhausted us all, we asked if he has a message for our entire Wiccan family. There are a few dozen of us now, all proudly tracing our lineage to Alex through Morven. He answered:

TO GET HERNES S

Morven puzzled over the response for a few seconds – spelling it out phonetically – it didn't make sense.

"To get Herne's S?" Morven questions, perhaps visualizing the Horned God of the Forest.

NO (This was a most emphatic "no")

"Alex, we don't understand, can you spell that again?" I ask. And the planchette moves patiently to the center of the board and begins to spell very slowly.

Morven copies every letter again, this time not trying to guess the spacing.

TOGETHERNESS

"Togetherness!" we call out simultaneously, laughing at how we could miss something so obvious.

And then he is gone.

I don't remember what happened next. We all kind of shuffled off to our tents mumbling to ourselves. What began as a game of amusement ended with the opening of a door onto the astral which provided a substantial glimpse of a man who had previously existed to me only in books and other people's anecdotes. Now Alex seemed very real to me. *He knew me, he spoke directly to me*. And the words that had tumbled out through the planchette rattled within my mind – *What books is he talking about? What is it we are supposed to know? Who's Fred?*

I climb into my sleeping bag and lay there for a long while before drifting off into a deep sleep.

"Togetherness," I whisper into the darkness.

And the only response comes from the great pine tree that sighs loudly above my head.

Chapter 2
Necromancy

It had been three months since the camping trip. The time went by quickly and there was little contact with any of the others. I thought of that night often, remembering (as I promised myself) the smell of the fire, the wavering light of the candles, and the cold earth beneath my feet. But mostly my thoughts were of Alex. His 'voice' haunted me, waking and sleeping, and I felt very strongly that if we tried again – he would return to us and continue his communication.

Raven and Jack invited me, along with Paul and Phoenix, to a Fall Equinox ritual and we accepted enthusiastically. It was an unbearably hot day and I found myself wandering through Raven's herb garden looking for a sheltered place to rest. I settled on an old stone wall beneath an apple tree and closed my eyes. The last days of summer swam back into consciousness. I remembered that before returning from the camping trip, we had built an altar in a secluded field to Lugh, the dying sun god, and invoked him in the final glorious days of the season of light.

"The sacrificial king," I sighed, and the face of Alex Sanders came into my mind so vividly that I nearly fell from the wall.

The ritual was seasonably appropriate but strangely unsettling to me. I was admittedly preoccupied, worrying about my familiar, a beautiful black cat whose health had been faltering in the previous weeks. Edgy during the feast, I was pulled aside by Raven who asked me what was wrong.

"No one has mentioned Alex", I said.

"Bring the Spirit Board at Samhain", she laughed, "We'll have a chat with him then."

I puzzled at this for a moment. As a witch, it seemed odd to relegate matters of spirit communication only to Halloween. But I let it drop and went home in a sullen mood to care for my dying cat. In fulfillment of my worst fears, he slipped away from me and was gone. I was devastated. We had spent twelve years together. It left me with an emptiness I found hard to shake.

"It is part of the season," I told myself, " Let it go."

Autumn came down fast and lingered. The leaves on the trees in the Boston Common changed color quickly and then hung for days on the wet branches – they turned and moved in the slightest breeze but would not fall. I watched them from the window of my office – trying to concentrate on business. It was nearly impossible, for the tide of All-Hallows was rising from the earth like a flood and it threatened to pull me in head-first if I wasn't careful.

The messages from Alex had been delivered safely to those he had chosen. There were mixed emotions – from stunned silence, to tears, to denial perhaps, to the most delirious joy. Even today, as I try to concentrate on other people's business, I ponder my own message. Alex had told me to "study". Or so I thought, for in the darkness he had spelled out "s-t-u-d" and the planchette had faltered. Someone called out "study" and the planchette moved to "yes". My message was certainly less spiritual than many of the others I had been asked to deliver. But I took it to a humble heart and resolved to study more than ever the ways of the Craft. I loved books and collected them relentlessly. They were stacked everywhere in my small apartment. But I bought them faster than I could read them. Perhaps Alex, the perpetual scholar, was prompting me to become more diligent in my approach to learning.

The phone on my desk rings loudly, pulling me out of my own private thoughts. It is Paul.

"Two days," he says flatly. I look at my desk calendar. It is October 29. "Are we still on for that dinner party?" We have devised a code of language that is appropriate for business environments.

"Wouldn't miss it," I laugh "Did you remember to invite Alex?"

"Oh yes, I hope he can make it. It's been a while since we've spoken with him."

We speak for a few moments more and then say goodbye.

Food for the dead, I scribble on a slip of paper and then, as an after-thought, I write beneath it *coffee and eggs*. I tuck it into my shirt pocket. "One stop grocery shopping," I think aloud and make a mental note to stop at the market on the way home.

Paul, Phoenix and I have decided to attempt to contact Alex again through the ancient rite of necromancy. We are a confident coven and our group soul is strong. We anticipate that we will be successful. We can sense Alex nearby, waiting patiently for an opportunity to finish that Lammas conversation. I make a silent promise to Alex that he will always be welcome in our circles. And as sure as a phoenix, in the last days of October, the power of the Craft rises again in my heart like a dark flame.

It is an hour or so before midnight on October 31, 1998. I gather my ritual tools into a worn backpack and walk the few blocks to Phoenix and Paul's apartment. The urban landscape is noisy with revelers. They brush past me in twos and threes, gather in the brightly- lit doorways of buildings, and wait on line in costume to enter the neighborhood bar.

"We each keep the season in our own way," I muse.

Paul greets me at the door and I enter the darkened apartment. Phoenix is lighting the quarter candles – the smell of incense hangs heavily. They are already robed and I quickly shed my mundane clothing and pull on my ritual robe. I meet them in the kitchen where Paul is putting the finishing touches on the Dumb Supper, a traditional feast which is offered to the Dead. I have baked bread and add it to the platter of food on the table.

We do not speak. Our mutual sense of purpose is obvious. I glance at the clock on the kitchen wall –

it presses on toward the witching hour and we silently resolve to begin. A ceremonial circle is marked out on the living room floor. An altar is ready on the western edge of this circle. It contains four plates, four chalices, a vase of red roses, and a photograph of Alex. We have placed around it our *Books of Shadows*, copied by hand from our initiators, as is Alexandrian tradition. A censer of necromantic incense burns steadily. We made the incense together at the last Full Moon – the complex ingredients included three drops of blood – one from each of us. With one heart, we begin to prepare the temple.

"Before us Raphael," Paul intones.

"Behind us Gabriel," I add solemnly. I am facing the altar we have built for Alex and above it hangs a large black mirror. Oddly, it does not reflect any of us and I make a mental note to share this with the others afterward.

"On our right hand Michael", Phoenix says strongly, "On our left hand Uriel."

The ritual continues as planned. Each word, each gesture is loaded with our intent.

"I invoke ye angels of the celestial spheres," Phoenix is saying, "Whose dwelling is in the invisible. Ye are the guardians of the gates of the universe. Be ye also the guardians of the gates of this mystic sphere."

As we begin to raise the ancient tide of power, it seems as if we transcend the confines of a Boston apartment and are standing within a temple so vast that the parameters of it blur into imagination. Our candles flame brightly against the dark and our voices resonate confidently in the still hour of midnight.

Paul is walking backward, in the way of the dead, carrying our incense and two white candles into the west. He kneels before the photo of Alex and lights the tapers from the western candle. Alex's face seems to leap into animation from within the glass frame. Phoenix follows in the same manner – he carries red wine. Finally, I follow, moving slowly in the same backward manner – bearing our solemn supper – pale cheese, freshly baked bread, apples, and clusters of purple grapes.

We wait for a few moments before continuing. My heart seems ready to jump out of my chest. I am anxious. I sense the others are as well. Finally, Paul breaks the tension and takes a single rose from the vase. He lays it across Alex's plate and says quietly:

"I welcome you, Alex Sanders, King of the Witches. Be with us now."

Phoenix fills Alex's chalice to overflowing with the wine. It sparkles in the candlelight and stains the white tablecloth beneath.

"I welcome you, Alex Sanders, our spiritual father. Be with us now."

I take small amounts of food and arrange them next to the rose. "Spirit of Alex Sanders," I continue, my voice wavering. "You may now approach the gates of the West. Arise, arise, I charge you. Be with us now."

I look into the mirror above our heads, which hangs directly over Alex's plate. It is foggy, a mist swirls across the surface.

"Spirit of Alex Sanders deceased, you may now pass beyond the gates of the West and enter our circle. Arise, arise, I charge you. Be with us now. We welcome you, Alex Sanders, by the ties of love that bind us, to break your eternal fast and sup with us. So mote it be!"

In the months that follow this evening, we would all have different memories of what happened next. Paul describes looking down and seeing Alex physically standing before him.

"I saw his bare feet and the hem of a white robe, trimmed with gold. He was as solid as we were. I did not feel as if I should look up into his face so I just stared at his feet. He stood just inside of the circle."

Phoenix saw him in the black mirror – he stood in the forefront of a crowd of other departed souls. "The ritual attracted many other spirits," he would tell me afterward, "They all wanted to come inside. Alex stood in the front of the crowd – he looked right at me."

I was glad that I had followed my instincts and decided to take an added precaution at the last minute. We had agreed that we would not breach the circle in any way. Although it seemed inappropriate to command Alex's spirit into the traditional *triangle of manifestation* used in necromancy, it seemed equally unwise to cut the circle to allow Alex to enter. We believed strongly that Alex would be capable of transcending our magickal boundary. Because of the other spirits, this proved to be a good decision.

I sensed Alex come into the circle and take his seat at the feast. I do remember that Paul was acting strangely. He kept staring at the floor and would not look up. Phoenix noticed this also and looked at me inquisitively.

"He shuddered," I would later comment. "His whole body convulsed for a second. It was as if Alex passed *through him* when he entered the circle."

We sat in silence for a while, each communing with Alex in our own quiet way and then Phoenix suggested we try the Spirit Board again. Paul and I took the planchette. Phoenix acted as scribe. Although no questions had been asked yet, the planchette moved quickly to:

YES

"Do you have a message for us? A spell to teach us?" Phoenix asks. He would later remark that he sensed that Alex wanted to instruct us in some manner of the occult.

F L Y   YES

"A flying spell?" Jimahl asks nervously "How? We are earthbound. How can we learn to fly?"

D Y E

The attempt to spell "die" leaves us all feeling a little weird. Of course we had walked in the path of the dead and were clearly out of our usual element. Then I ask something like:

"Alex, are you making a joke? Are you saying that to learn a flying spell you must die?"
The planchette moves weakly and spells:

S E E R S   Y E S

"Do you want to teach us to be Seers?"

NO   D J I N

Phoenix, remembering the camping retreat, asks if Alex is referring to scrying by fire.

YES   C A U L D R O N

"Alex, are you saying this is a good time to invoke the element of fire for scrying?"

YES

Paul and I stare at each other across the board. He seems distant and I start to worry that we are all too tired to be doing this type of thing. Alex feels different this time, as if the connection is very strained. There is a heavy feeling in the air – like we are wrapped in wet fabric.

"Alex," I press on, "Can you tell us more about the messages you gave us at Lammas?"

HEED THEM WELL   YES

"Alex, I need some clarification on my message. You started to spell a word but did not finish."

YES

"Was the word *study*?"

The planchette moves painfully slow now and Alex begins to spell:

S T U D ...   Then to my surprise, the completed word expands to:

S T U D E N T S

"Students!" I laugh out loud, realizing how I had spent three months contemplating an erroneous message. "My *current* students?" I ask, meaning Paul and Phoenix.

NO   MO R E

"Alex, I am finished teaching for now. My students now have students. I need a break."

NO T A K E M O R E
I H A D   H U N D R E D S   YES

This is a humbling response. I am speechless.

"Alex," Paul asks "Your message to me was to 'heal others'. How can I do this?"

HANDS

"Alex, I have had no experience with healing. How can I heal with my hands?"

TOUCH

"You're saying this is my spiritual talent?"

YES

"Is there anything else Alex?" Paul asks.

NO

"Did you enjoy the supper?" I ask.

YES ABSORB

And then without warning the planchette moves to:

GOODBYE

At this point we all feel him leave. The circle seems to grow immediately colder. I sense a familiar draft about my ankles that always comes as the power wanes.

We each retrace the path of the dead, moving this time out of the realm of the departed into the world of the living.

As we inhabit the last vestiges of our Samhain circle, I thank Alex for hearing our call and invoke the Most Ancient Goddess into our temple.

"Oh Mighty Mother," I pray, "Wake the witch in us. Set a fire ablaze in our hearts for the love of the Craft. Empower us with your Dark Magick!"
Paul is standing next to me. He smiles and nods. Phoenix embraces me and says, "Now *that* was a ritual to remember! I think we've all earned a beer!"

The next morning I awake to the sound of the telephone. It is Phoenix.

"Paul is very sick," he says urgently, "Can you come over here *now*? I don't know what to do."

Because Phoenix is not the type of individual who gets easily excited, I realize Paul's situation must be extremely grave. I dress rapidly and run the few blocks to their apartment.

"Thanks for coming," Phoenix says. "I didn't know who else to call."

I enter the dark apartment. Although it is a bright morning, the shades are all drawn. It takes a moment for my eyes to adjust.

"Where is he?" I ask. Phoenix points to Paul's bedroom door, which is closed. "What's wrong with him?"

"I don't know. We stayed up a while last night after you left. He seemed to be fine. But this morning he won't get out of bed."

I walk to the bedroom door and knock once. There is no answer. I push the door open and walk into the room. Many years previously I had worked as a security guard in a hospital. I remembered clearly the curious smell prevalent in the rooms of terminally ill patients. It was a sweet dark smell – like flowers on the ebb. I was startled to smell it now – filling Paul's bedroom. He lies under a thin sheet, which is pulled up to just below his chest. The first thing I notice is that he is so pale – his flesh is the color of day old snow. He has a cloth over his eyes and if he noticed me enter the room, he does not acknowledge my presence. Phoenix comes in behind me and looks at me expectantly. It was at times like this that I wished desperately for an official *High Priest Manual* to consult. So much of the occult had to be learned the hard way.

"Paul," I whisper "Can you hear me?"

"I hurt," he says faintly. His voice raises the hair on the back of my neck. It is *not* his voice.

"Every part of me hurts. I feel like I'm dying."

"You're not dying. What's wrong?"

"I don't understand," he says in a raspy voice. "I have never been this sick in my life."

I look at Phoenix who stares back at me. My mind flashes quickly on the previous evening.

"We did everything right," I murmur. "By the book. What could have gone wrong?" I then somehow instinctively knew what was wrong, but denial felt pretty good at that particular moment.

"Let's get him into the living room," I say to Phoenix.

We move to either side of Paul and try to get him out of the bed. He stands up weakly, wavering on his ankles like he's about to break into pieces. We half- walk, half-drag him into the living room and lay him down in the center of the floor.

"Get some pillows for his head," I instruct Phoenix.

I wrestle with the shades on the windows and the unapologetic light washes the room. Paul moans and covers his eyes with his hands.

Paul, usually as solid and fit as a young Viking, lies on the bare floor clad only in a pair of gray shorts. His blond hair is streaked with sweat, his blue eyes clouded. I am in an adrenaline rush right now. I have no idea what is physically wrong with my friend but my hunch is that it has something to do with Alex. I glance at my watch and figure I have a ten-minute window to try to right things before I suggest to Phoenix that we call an ambulance.

"Bring the salt and water from the altar," I say to Phoenix, who does not seem to mind my direction. I begin to bathe Paul's feet with the consecrated water from our ritual. His body seems to wither as each painful moment slips by.

"This is an illusion," I tell Phoenix, "This isn't really happening. Bathe his forehead with the consecrated water." Phoenix does so and still I watch the flesh on Paul's body pull taut – I can see every rib now. I am on the verge of panic. I try to remember every detail of the ritual. *Something went wrong*, I think silently. Then I recall what happened at the moment Alex came into the circle. Paul had shuddered involuntarily – his whole body shook. Instinctively, I knew that Paul had not only been the watcher of the western gate – he had inadvertently *become the gate*. Alex had passed *through him* into the circle.

"Think," I say to Phoenix. "What do we know about necromancy?"

"Historically it was used to reanimate the corpse," Phoenix says. I can see his concern for Paul's health is accelerating.

"Right, but we knew that wasn't going to be the case with Alex. So we raised his spirit – not in hypothetical form – but his actual *ghost* – for lack of a better word."

"Get to the point," Phoenix says urgently, "What do we do now?"

"I think Alex literally passed into Paul and then through him into the circle. But some aspect of Alex remains there."

"Remains where?" Phoenix asks impatiently.
I nod in Paul's direction. "In there – inside Paul."
"So what do we do?"

"Alex, we love you and honor you," I say. "But we realize that somehow a part of your spirit became lodged in Paul's body. This is causing Paul's body to take on the physical form you knew in the last hours of your life. He is reliving your illness, Alex. He is feeling your pain. You have to help us, Alex." Paul begins to cry – great heaving sobs that shake his whole body. Suddenly his torso, from chest to toe, is raised from the floor and bent backward like a bow.

"Alex, for the love of the Goddess, let go of Paul now!"

Paul's body slams back to the floor with a thud.

He lies there for a few minutes and then opens his eyes and looks directly at me. I recognize the familiar light there.

"Let's just stick with the Spirit Board," he says, and we all laugh.

CHAPTER THREE

THE SECOND GROUP SESSION

It was a week later and the three of us were together again – this time in Paul's car heading out of Boston toward Raven and Jack's covenstead. If the leaves on the trees in the city were reluctant to fall, just the opposite was true in the suburbs north of town. The wet branches showed little signs of life and the landscape was distinctly uninviting. A low ground fog rose up on either side of the two-lane blacktop and added to the dreary atmosphere. Paul inched up the steep hill that leads to the covenstead, his high-beams barely illuminating the pavement ahead of us.

"A great night for a ghost hunt," Phoenix joked. The evening promised to be entertaining. Raven and Jack own one of the most haunted houses in New England. Four ghosts had been documented there to date – one of whom we had encountered at Lammas. The other resident spirits included a mysterious gardener (never seen inside the house but always anxious to dispense gardening advice to unsuspecting guests on the patio), an energetic two- year old named Edward, and the spirit of a woman who frequently awakened house guests in the morning by calling out their names.

Because so many members of our Wiccan family had young children who enjoyed trick or treating, this annual ritual was deliberately scheduled a week past actual Halloween to facilitate attendance.

"Is everyone going to be there?" I ask from the back seat, where I am surrounded by pillows and sleeping bags. Since the ritual was scheduled to begin at midnight, Raven suggested we sleep over afterward.

"I think we'll have a full house," Paul responds, still focusing intently on the foggy highway. "I got last-minute emails from five of them reminding me to bring the Spirit Board."

"I hope Alex will join us," I respond. There was a moment of silence and I realize we are all thinking of the Necromancy experiment.

"So what the hell happened last weekend?" Phoenix finally asks.

"I think it should have been an expected side effect. I suppose there is an inherent danger of possession in any spirit work." I had given the situation some thought in the last few days.

"Possession?" Paul laughs nervously.

"I don't mean possession in a head-spinning way," I explain, "But I think it's somewhat natural for disembodied spirits to gravitate toward a warm body."

"Like the impulse to get in out of the cold," Phoenix said.

"Exactly," I continue. "But the fact that Alex sort of hung around with Paul for a while could be symptomatic of something else."

The farmhouse floats into view suddenly as Paul's vehicle rounds the top of the steep hill. Set against a field of night, the lights of the many windows glow like the eyes of a huge jack-o-lantern. Paul parks the car at the edge of a crowded driveway and turns off the engine. We sit there for a moment in the dark.

"You were saying?" Paul smiles.

"Just call it a hunch. But I don't think Alex has passed through the veil. I assumed he was speaking to us from the other side. But now I think his spirit may still be earthbound."

The front door of the house swings open and from across the yard a blade of yellow light illuminates the flag stone path. A cloaked figure moves toward us. We step out into the cold November air.

The sound of a violin surprises us, drifting thickly upon the wind. Raven throws her arms up to greet us.

"Welcome, welcome," she says, her long black hair blows in the wind. Her cat circles her ankles. We make our way into the house quickly and shut the door against the dampness.

A vigorous fire is blazing in the massive stone hearth and the music of the violin fills the room completely.

Sulis is standing in front of the fire, her back as straight as a door, the instrument cradled against her chin, her head thrown back in the rapture of the music. Her long red hair falls over her shoulders and dances like the flames on the hearth. The music is passionate, sad in a way, but only in that enigmatic way that makes one happy to be sad. She sways from side to side as she plays, lost in the bittersweet notes that she alone creates. When she finishes with a flourish, there is applause and warm words from the others.

"Jimahl," she calls out when she sees me, and we kiss.

The house takes the three of us in quickly, embracing us as only an old house can. Morven is there, looking radiant in the firelight, curled elegantly onto the edge of the sofa. Jack comes into the room from the kitchen carrying a large bowl of candy in his strong hands.

"Leftovers from last weekend," he laughs.

I pass by him and enter the kitchen. The aromas that drift from the oven are intoxicating - sweet cinnamon, crisp apple, and the smell of baking bread. A pot of stew simmers on top of the cast iron stove. Willow stands over it with a wooden spoon.

"I could use some rosemary," she says as I enter. I take a few pinches of the herb from bunches of drying plants that hang in front of Raven's antique china cabinet. Willow accepts the ingredient from me and drops it into the mixture.

"Rosemary for remembrance," she smiles.

"I was hoping you'd be here," I say as I embrace her warmly. She leans into me, her body is as soft as a pillow.

I consider Willow to be my Wiccan sister. We became students to Morven at the same time and grew into the Craft together. Just as two trees, planted beside each other, may appear to be independent above the ground and yet share unseen roots below the ground, so was my relationship with Willow inexplicably intertwined. After years spent walking the same path, life circumstances eventually separated us. It had been a year or more since we stood in the same room. Willow sighs loudly. Willow speaks volumes in her sighs. She is the living embodiment of the axiom *still waters run deep*.

Ruanna comes into the kitchen from the back yard. She is younger in the Craft than Willow and myself, having come to Morven for instruction much later.

There is an aura of antiquity to Ruanna. Witchcraft seems to cover her like a mantle and she wears it well. A scarlet tattoo of a rising sun is etched beautifully over her heart.

"We're all set up in the carriage house," she announces. "We've just got to get a few more logs in the wood burning stove. It's cold out there."

As if on cue, Morph comes in from the living room carrying an armload of firewood.

"Did someone mention wood?" he laughs. Perhaps it is the magician's robe, its hem dotted with stars and moons – but Morph seems to me like a young Merlin tonight. He is perhaps the most intellectual person I know. He is found, more often than not, settled into a comfortable chair with a good book in his lap and his eyeglasses balanced precariously on the end of his nose.

"Is everyone here?" Ruanna asks. "It's getting close to midnight." There is the sound of footsteps again in the foyer and a fresh round of "hellos".

It is Tanith. She is the true elder among us, having been instrumental in the training of Morven. Tanith is ageless in the way that most Wiccan women become – with features as fine as porcelain and long, slender hands that seem to weave patterns in the air when they move.

"What a warm welcome," Tanith says, as she patiently hugs each one of us. "Oh dear, there are so many of you. How exciting! Happy Samhain, Blessed Be!"

When all have settled again, Raven announces that it is time to begin the ritual. We drift off into adjoining rooms to complete our individual preparations. I robe quickly, and draw a black cloak around my shoulders. The others have already started to form a procession. I join them and together we move silently from the warmth of the living room, through the bright kitchen, and out of the heavy door that leads to the rear of the house. We cross the broad expanse of wet grass in our bare feet, our cloaks and robes billow in the wind.

The door of the carriage house is open – candlelight beckons invitingly from inside. We enter quickly and the door is shut behind us. It takes a moment for my eyes to adjust to the dim light. A large circle is drawn out on the planked floor. An altar, overflowing with produce from Raven's garden, is set up at the edge of this circle. There are candles everywhere, set around the perimeter of the space – spilling lavishly across the altar, and flickering slyly from inside carved pumpkins, which ring the room like enchanted sentinels. An old pot-bellied stove dominates one corner of the renovated space. The heat from the stove fogs the windows and makes the rough wooden floor warm beneath our feet. The smell of the burning hardwood is a heady incense.

"As the wheel of the year slows, the cycle of change pulls us into dark, cool spaces," Jack proclaims as he walks slowly around the circle. "The leaves fall from the trees – orange and red – to the earth below where they become as we all must become – dust - a part of the dark wet void from which surges the cosmic impulse of regeneration."

We join hands and begin to dance slowly– swaying from side to side as Morph keeps time on a hollow drum.

"Dark Lady," Jack invokes, "By want so keen, it cuts like knife. By heart of green as sharp as scythe. I call thee forth, O Queen of Night. By waning light of silver moon, by breath of night I chant this rune. By darkness deep I know thee nigh. By wind and rain and lowering sky. By circle round we weave your spell. Shake and shudder, shriek and scream, Phantom Mother, Shadow Queen."

Raven appears suddenly in the shadows of the altar. She wears a dark red veil, which hangs low across her face.

"This is the time for scrying," she says, "For looking into black mirrors and divining with the Tarot. The veil between the living and the dead is lifted for a moment. Let us now commune with those who have gone before. Let us see our own future in the shadows between the worlds."

As we sprawl out in the center of the large circle, a mutual excitement begins to build. Although there are plenty of runes, tarot cards, and dark crystal spheres to utilize, Raven suggests Paul and myself try to contact Alex on the Spirit Board. The board is brought out and we all sit around it.

Morven volunteers to act as Scribe. Most of what follows was adapted directly from her notes.

"We would like to speak to the spirit of Alex Sanders." I say, my voice echoing in the rafters.

S O R L B D R

"We would like to talk to Alex Sanders," I repeat.

B O R R E E

"Alex, are you there?"

C R T A H

At this point it is clear we aren't getting anything, so we release the planchette. I am feeling very anxious and wonder if we will be successful.

"That wasn't him," Paul states. "It's just nonsense."

"Try again," Morven encourages.

"We only want to talk to Alex Sanders. Alex, are you there?" I ask.

YES

The planchette wasn't moving in the way that I had come to understand as Alex. There was an odd feeling in the air. Still, I persisted. "If this is you Alex, what do you have to say to us tonight?"

H E L O G R A T D H B L B R U

Raven says sternly, "Tell the two-year old to leave."

"Is this the little boy who lives here?" I ask, referring to the child who haunts the hallways of the farmhouse.

EDWARD

"Edward, is that you?" Raven asks.

YES

"We'll contact you some other time. You have to go now." To my surprise, Raven speaks to the child's spirit in the firm, but loving, tone of a mother. The child responds with one last flourish of nonsense and then is gone.

We decide to try Alex again.

"Alex, are you here?" According to Morven's notes, I am asking most of the questions this time.

YES

"What do you have to say to us?"

K N O W L UV YES

"Alex, do you know anyone in this room?"

YES

"Do you know us all?"

NO

"Who do you not know?"

HINT

" Do you know Sulis?"

YES

"Do you know Ruanna?"

YES

"Alex, will you speak to us tonight?"

HI TANITH

Tanith looks up in surprise from the edge of the circle. She had spent some time with Alex when he was alive. "Long time, no see, Alex."

GODES LUVS U

"Oh, thank you, Alex!" Tanith beams.

HELO THN ASK

"You want us to ask you questions?" I say expectantly.

YES

The excitement in the Circle begins to build. Morph calls out from across the room.

"Do you know me, Alex?"

To our surprise, Alex acknowledges his question by spelling out Morph's *mundane name.*

Alex, then, spells: **S U L I S**

"Yes, Alex, I'm here," Sulis responds.

I see Willow stir out of the corner of my eye. Although she was given a message from Alex at Lammas, she had not yet had the opportunity of speaking with him directly.

"Do you know me?" Willow asks shyly.

KEEP TRUE TO YOR ART

"Do you mean the Wiccan Craft?" she pursues.

NO

"Do you mean my work as an artist?"

Willow is an accomplished illustrator.

YES

"Is there a piece of art you want me to do?" she asks.

WOMAN

"Any particular woman?"

GODES

Willow smiles broadly and glances at me. The others begin to think of more questions.

"Anything for me, Alex?" Phoenix says.

DREAM SPEL

"I'll dream a spell?"

YES

"Alex, when I scry with fire, is that the salamanders' realm?"

MAYBE

"What can you tell Sulis about her group?" Morven asks. Sulis had been training students of her own for a few years now.

E L D R S

It is an appropriate response. Each of Sulis' three students had recently been elevated to Second Degree Alexandrian. In our tradition they were now considered to be Elders of the Craft.

"Any messages for Jack or me?" Raven asks quietly.

S T O P   W O R R Y I N G

This elicits laughter from the couple so I assume Alex's comment makes sense to them.

"Any messages for me?" Morph is now wide-eyed and anxious. He, too, had only experienced Alex's first communication second-hand.

M A G I C I A N   YES

We thought this was significant because Morph was very interested in Ceremonial Magick.

"Anything for me?" Ruanna asks.

OPEN HEART

"Anything for me Alex?" Paul whispers. I know he is getting tired, as am I. The planchette has been moving very energetically.

HANDS

"Should I study holistic massage?" Paul's previous messages from Alex have been about the gift of healing.

YES WELL

"To make others well?"

YES

"Anything for me, Alex?" I ask. I can feel the energy really begin to wane now.

STUDENTS

"I know, Alex, you've had hundreds!" I laugh. "I hear you. I understand."

"Am I ever going to feel I'm competent to teach?" Morph asks.

YES

"When should I start?"

N O W   G R O W

"Teaching others will make me grow?"

YES

"Are you serious about your rebirth in the year 2000?" Raven asks.

YES

"Do you have to, or do you choose to?"

L O N E L Y

"Will you be born to someone within our coven family?" Morven inquires.

NO

"Will it be in England?"

NO

"Will your mother be Wiccan?"

YES

"Will we know you again?"

IN TIME

"Do you have anything else to say, Alex?" I realized it must be very late. We had cast the Circle at the stroke of midnight and the candles in the pumpkins had been out for a while now.

YES GROW

Morven would later write:

At this time, Paul and Jimahl break the communication, with Jimahl saying, "Thank you, Alex."

Alex's presence hung in the room for a long while. His words rang as clearly in all of our hearts as if he had stood physically among us, as if he had embraced each of us. In a way he had, for he did not fail to come to us when we asked for him. And the words he spoke to each of us seemed, as they had before, to reach the core of our spirit.

I remember the silence immediately after Paul and I let go of the planchette as being particularly noteworthy. We sat there on the floor of the carriage house, our robes drawn tight against the waxing chill. No one moved. I know we probably each were thinking the same thoughts, felt the same mixed emotions – it was as if we were one soul, one mind. That, in retrospect, was the magick of Alex Sanders.

When we did finally break the Circle and return to the farmhouse dining room to share our late night feast, there seemed to be a renewed sense of hope in each of us. Samhain, after all, was the time of the year to acknowledge death as not an ending, but another beginning.

Alex, deceased for ten years now, was still among us. He cared about us. He encouraged us to grow and to become closer than ever before. He challenged us to live the Craft every day and to share the mysteries with new students. How perfect it all seemed.

And so we ended the evening by raising our glasses to him.

"Hail to the King of the Witches," we sang out.

"Thank you Alex," I whispered, "Thank you so much."

CHAPTER FOUR
DREAMS AND QUESTIONS

It is nearly four in the morning when I lie down on an overstuffed sofa in the den to sleep, but sleep will not come easily. An antique clock somewhere in the house chimes on the half-hour and keeps me tossing from side to side. Like a boat without an anchor, my mind drifts randomly on the ebb of consciousness bringing thoughts and images of Alex to the forefront. Question after question surfaces – most of them impossible to answer.

How could he still be earthbound ten years after his death? Was he being hindered in some way from passing over? Was he communicating in this way with anyone else? Should we tell others about this? Would they believe us if we did? Could we just be imagining the whole thing?

Again and again the questions come rising up out of the murky half-asleep mind and the clock in the other room keeps chiming. Eventually I resign myself to a sleepless night and position myself on the sofa to face a large window. I can see a slice of sky through the lace curtain – already beginning to lighten with dawn.

I awake an hour or so later with bright light on my face. It is still early and the rest of the house is quiet.

I had been dreaming of Alex. Or rather remembering, in a dream colored with nostalgia, a vision I had of Alex shortly after his death:

It was the first of May 1988. Unknown to me at the time, Alex had passed away the day before. I was new to the Craft then, having joined Morven's coven in early April. Morven had sent Alex news of the coven's formation. It was the last communication Alex and Morven would have, and quite likely one of the final pieces of Craft news he would receive prior to his death.

I had gotten up just before dawn – which wasn't unusual for me – and gone into the living room of my suburban apartment I was living in at the time. Alex Sanders was standing in the center of the room. He was dressed in a white ceremonial robe.

Having had some experience with lucid dreaming prior to this experience, I resolved that I was still asleep and made an effort to stay in the subconscious state as long as possible.

"Bring me your tools," Alex said to me. I only had two magickal objects to call my own at that time. The first was my athame, the traditional double-edged knife used in witchcraft. The second was a blank book I had chosen as a future *Book of Shadows*. I would soon copy into it by hand all of the rituals and spells passed down to me by my teacher.

I did as he asked and brought the two humble items to him. Laying his hands on the book and the athame, Alex blessed them and encouraged me to be true to the Craft. He said that I would succeed with my studies and contribute significantly to the perpetuation of Alexandrian Wicca.

"Remember me," he said, "Leave a chair for me in all your circles. Tell the others."

I received a call from Morven much later in the day stating that Alex had died the day before. I told her about my experience hesitantly. I was self-conscious that she or the others might think it presumptuous to believe that the *King of the Witches* had visited me personally.

Morven took the information to heart and for many months after there was an empty chair next to the altar in every circle we cast. It was understood that this chair was there for Alex if he should choose to visit our circle. But the chair eventually became much more than a token of remembrance – it became a symbol of our own commitment to the Craft.

The chair reminded us that since Alex Sanders was no longer incarnate, *we were now responsible* for keeping his tradition intact. The chair became an icon for a sacred trust, one that weighed heavily on our hearts and minds. And ultimately, one that would deeply influence each of our lives in the years ahead.

A noise above my head brings me back to the present. There is a creaky tread down the wooden staircase and Paul and Phoenix come into the room. Paul, too, has dreamed of Alex and is anxious to share his experience:

"I lay awake for a long time listening to the house settle around me. There are so many noises in an old house that you don't hear in an apartment building. Eventually I must have dozed off. I remember opening my eyes and seeing Alex standing over the bed. He was wearing the same white robe with the gold trim. He took my hand and brought me downstairs. I remember looking at myself and thinking that I shouldn't be wondering around someone else's house in my underwear. It was that real. We went into the living room. I saw you asleep on the sofa. Alex and I sat down in front of the fireplace and talked. There was a fire burning there – the room was very warm. I don't remember everything he told me, but one thing in particular stands out. He said that a great truth would be revealed to me in a dream. The sense of being face to face with him was very clear."

Phoenix said that he was given a "dream spell" during the night, exactly as Alex had mentioned in the previous Spirit Board session. It was a spell utilizing the element of fire. An extremely competent magician, Phoenix was especially adept at raising and directing dragon energy.

The others are waking one by one and moving around above our heads. We move into the chilly kitchen of the farmhouse and are delighted to see that Raven had set up the coffee service the night before. As the coffee brews, we sit around the kitchen table in fuzzy silence.

There seems to be a big question hanging over our heads – like one of those blurbs in a cartoon drawing. It is a question that none of us are prepared to answer: *Now what do we do?*

The smell of the coffee drifts through the house, summoning everyone to breakfast. Soon we are all participating in a lively discussion over a banquet of breakfast foods. I turn the subject intentionally to Alex.

Willow seems particularly disturbed and voices her concerns the loudest.

"I don't understand why he wants to reincarnate in the year 2000. We've just made contact with him. What's the hurry?"

"We still have more than a year," Morven reasons. "We'll use the time we have left wisely."

"But why do we have to race against the clock? It doesn't make sense. If this is Alex, he'd want to give us as much of his time as possible."

"Maybe it's not his fault that it took ten years for someone to make contact with him," I interject. "Imagine being around for a decade, standing in the background, just waiting."

Willow persists, "But look at the statement he made about being *lonely*. How can he be lonely? There's got to be a lot of Wiccans on the other side."

"I don't think he's on the other side," I say flatly. "I think he's earthbound."

"Earthbound? You mean he never passed over? Never went anywhere? Just stepped out of his body and hung around?" Willow was clearly distraught. I understood why the subject of death caused her so much pain. A close friend had been seriously ill for years and was quickly losing ground. It would have been far more reassuring if Alex spoke of the afterlife as a land of enchantment and unending joy.

"Sort of like a ghost," Ruanna volunteers.

"Yes," I say emphatically. "Exactly like a ghost."

"But why do spirits hang around," Raven asks. "Do you suppose it could be unfinished business?"

"I don't know," I admit. "Perhaps it was a decision he made when he died. Maybe he wanted to stay around for a while. I remember reading a letter he published just before he died. It said something like 'soon I will be with you all'. Maybe he meant it literally."

"But *ten years*," Willow shakes her head, "I don't get it."

That morning, over the bagels and cream cheese, there was clearly a nerve struck in our group soul that would resonate painfully over the months of darkness that lay ahead. It was impossible for us to know at the time that we would never have the opportunity to speak to Alex as a group again. If we had known this, perhaps we would have shoved the junk food aside and brought out the Spirit Board one more time. Perhaps we would have spoken with Alex until all of our questions were answered. But there was a certain level of apathy within the group that I found disconcerting. It was as if there was this elephant in the kitchen. And no one wanted to acknowledge the elephant. This was Alex, *King of the Witches*. He had proven twice now that he was available to us. We could ask him anything. We could talk about the Craft and the Mysteries of the Goddess. We could ask him the most intimate questions about his life. We could ask him why it was that he was compelled to remain between the worlds for over a decade - what pressing business did he leave unfinished?

But instead the conversation shifted to the weather, our children, and plans for the winter holidays ahead.

After a while, we pack up the cars and get ready to head home. I am quiet and Paul asks what is wrong.

"I understand why Alex is so lonely."

CHAPTER FIVE

DESCENT INTO WINTER

There was little contact with most of the others over the next few months. The days grew shorter and the nights longer. The cold weather came down like a curtain. As a pagan and a witch, I had grown accustomed to these seasonal tides. I understood that winter represented the season of darkness – a time when the inherent powers of growth and reanimation went underground. This was the time of the year for introspection, for quiet solitude, a cosmic opportunity for "time-out." But this year the descent of winter also brought problems. I would later comment, when the world again was poised on the brink of Spring, that the winter of 1998 had been the darkest I had ever known. I am sure this sentiment was also true for many of my immediate Wiccan family.

In retrospect, it became evident that the words Alex had spoken to each of us in the bright days of summer were prophetic in nature. If he spoke of "learning laughter," it became evident that a heart-rending tragedy was looming on the horizon. If he spoke of the need for "healing," it foreshadowed sickness and depression that would dominate the months ahead. If he admonished us to stay "together," it foreshadowed a time when the bonds of our friendship would be tested beyond our comprehension.

I reflected continually on the events of the previous months. Morven meticulously transcribed each of the sessions and emailed them to everyone. I pored over the notes again and again looking for a clue as to Alex's expectations. There was a nagging feeling in my heart that preempted every other thought – Alex had more on his agenda than just stopping by to say hello on the way to the afterlife. There was something else he needed to say – something he needed to accomplish – and he was incapable of doing it alone.

At one point, I would write in my journal:

"If only there were adequate words to say exactly what it is that I want to say – perhaps if I could explain how heavily the thoughts of Alex weigh on my mind the others would understand. There is not a moment that I don't sense him waiting in the darkness – just out of reach – where he has likely been for years. The forest from which he first spoke to us has taken on a deeper meaning. No longer representative of only the campground in New Hampshire, the forest now must also be seen as a metaphor for the wilderness that lies between life and death. The wild place that Alex inhabits – described in his own words as "lonely" – is the embodiment of all that humans dread. It is the great unknown. No wonder we are disturbed by the idea of death. It is the one mystery that no man has solved. We can accept the business of living, for that is what we are good at – the calendar and the ticking clock are our best friends. We are carried forward from one life event to another. Our children are born and as they grow we see our youth in their reflections. They immortalize us. They preserve us. The house and the yard and the seasons of life and death and rebirth as reflected in the seasons of the year – are all manageable microcosms of loss and renewal. We can accept that the snow will fall and cover the earth only because we know that sooner or later the green will emerge again from the ice. But when a loved one looks at us for the last time, there are no words to describe how terrified we are. There are pictures out of books and stories that we tell each other about angels of light and the spirits of those who have gone before who will welcome us over when our time comes. There are doctors who can wrap us in numb abeyance so that the pain is a negligent side-effect. There is the faith of a thousand religions and the faces of a thousand Gods that all basically say the same thing – no one really knows! And whatever it is that we need to believe, we embrace. In the face of death it is as natural as breathing to hold on to life. We resolve to face our end bravely when our time comes. We promise to be strong for those who depend on us for strength in crisis. But the bottom line is always the same. No one knows what happens in that final moment. I can understand, then, why a voice from the other side can inadvertently cause mixed emotions. To acknowledge that voice immediately takes us where we do not want to go. To hear that voice, we have to move beyond the world of the living and put ourselves in an unfamiliar space. This is a predictably frightening situation. And yet I see Alex in that forest every time I close my eyes. He is standing in the shadows, his face turned expectantly toward me. *How deep are those woods, Alex? How far away have you gone to be so near?"*

I will be the first to admit that I was becoming obsessed with Alex. I could not stop thinking about him. I was unable to relegate his few communications to the realm of happenstance. I sensed that there was work to do, mysteries to unravel, questions to be asked – and that somehow my *personal involvement* was necessary. A bond developed between Alex and me that defied explanation. If I closed my eyes, I saw him. When I slept, I dreamed of him. I resolved to do whatever I could do to help him. I promised him that I would take this as far as I could – that I would unselfishly give until there was nothing more I could give.

Morven listened patiently and agreed that there was more to the situation than we originally thought. Always encouraging, always supportive, she urged me cautiously forward.

Paul and Phoenix spent hours with me – searching through old books and notes – scouring volumes of occult literature for any mention of Alex Sanders.

A strong proponent of the "power in numbers" theory, I also called two other Wiccan friends, Asha and Finbar, into service. Although they had been absent each of the previous times Alex spoke, the personal messages that Alex sent to them had a profound impact on their lives.

"We would love to help," Asha said happily. "Anything you need, just let us know."

And so it was that in the last vestiges of winter, our faces were turned once more toward the promise of light.

January went by quickly and Candlemas was once again upon us. On February eve, Paul, Phoenix, and Morven joined me in my Boston apartment to celebrate the Sabbat.

The altar was adorned with white roses and shimmering mirrors. Tall white candles filled the room with fragile light.

Encouraged by the inevitable greening of the year, I invoked the Goddess of Winters End into our Circle.

"Between the snow and the equinox, we've many a road to wander. When gods pass by, we hear their voice in rain and wind and thunder. But we're never alone as we make our way home, for green is the path that leads us. When dark and light meet as one, the Lady will be there to greet us!"

At ritual's end we share a feast of white food – delicate cakes shaped like crescent moons, slivers of almonds and a chalice of pale wine.

Because we were anxious to speak again with Alex, we ate our ritual meal quickly. The Spirit Board was then set up in the center of the small room.

Morven took up a notebook and a pen and waited expectantly. Phoenix sat nearby with a digital camera. Paul and I set up the board and placed our hands on the familiar planchette. Dave, my life partner, was also present.

The room was still lit by candles. One of them was brought from the altar and placed over the board so that we could see the intricately carved letters.

"OK Alex," I thought silently, "you want to talk – we're listening. Let's go."

And as sure as the fact that Spring follows Winter, the planchette jumps into motion.

CHAPTER SIX

A LIGHT IN THE FOREST

The planchette moves quickly in erratic circles – covering the board again and again without stopping at any letters.

"We only want to speak with Alex Sanders." I state clearly. The planchette stops abruptly:

YES

"Alex, are we to understand this is you?"

M O R V E N

"Yes Alex. I'm here," she responds. "Will you speak with us again?"

YES

"Did you see our ritual tonight?" I ask

YES

"Do you know we think of you all the time?"

YES

There is a series of incomprehensible responses, followed by inactivity.

"Alex, is it difficult for you to communicate tonight?"

YES

" Why is that?"

I M F O G Y YES

"You're foggy tonight, Alex?"

YES

"Why is that?"

V E I L YES

"Maybe the veil is not that thin?" Phoenix suggests.

YES

"The veil is not thin between the worlds?"

YES D R I N K

"Is it because we've had something to drink tonight?" Morven asks.

NO

"Do *you* want something to drink?"

YES

"Where should we leave something for you to drink?"

W E S T

Morven would later note:

"We stop here to put some red wine in a glass and place it on a small table in the west. We know Alex prefers white, but we didn't want to stop long enough to open a bottle because we were afraid we'd lose him. At this point we also looked at the pictures Phoenix was taking with the digital camera. In the third one it looks like Alex's face is superimposed over Paul's face. As we're getting ready to restart, Paul notices small droplets of water on the planchette! There is no water nearby and no one is sweating."

"Alex," Morven continues, "We gave you some wine."

YES

"Did you have some?"

YES

"Alex, was that you superimposed over Paul's face?" I ask.

YES

"Do you come into him physically when we do these sessions?" I pursue.

YES

"Always Paul?"

YES

"Then what is my purpose?"

MEDIUM YES

"I'm a medium? So, what is Paul?"

CHANEL

"Paul is a channel?"

YES

"It takes two of us to contact you this way?"

YES

"Have I been a medium in a past life, Alex?"

YES

"Is it a talent I should I develop it in this life?"

YES

"Alex, is there anything else you want to say to us tonight?" Morven asks.

SEND BLESING YES

"Alex, those blessings come from you?"

YES

"Is there anything you want us to do?"

CARRY ON

"Alex," I say, "We're doing that. Does this make you happy?"

YES

"Alex, do you know about Paul and Phoenix's new students?"

YES PRIESTESSES

"Priestesses?" Paul remarks. He and Phoenix have recently begun to train three female students. Paul had commented to me previously that he sensed Alex's presence whenever they met with their students.

YES (And then another, more emphatic) **YES**

"Alex, am I a channel?" Paul asks.

YES

"Is this why I have health problems after these sessions?"

YES

"Can I control these problems?"

YES

"What should I do?"

WATER

"Drink it?"

YES

"Alex, do you have anything to say to Morven?"

He responds by spelling out her Third Degree name – a name he chose for her at Samhain.

"You like my name, Alex?"

C O N G R A T S YES

"Do you have anything for me?" Phoenix asks.

D R A G O N S S U R O U N D U YES

"Anything for me tonight, Alex?" I wonder aloud.

STUDENTS

"Alex, is this the same message as the last time we spoke?"

YES

"Where will I find them?"

U WILL FIND YES

"I'm learning healing, Alex," Paul interjects.

YES

There was a sudden down shift in the energy.

"Alex, your energy wanes," I state. "Would more wine help?"

NO

"Is it time to go?"

YES

I immediately wanted more. In my mind I asked him to stay, to talk to us, to help us understand what it was he needed.

IN TIME

"In time?" I ask, surprised that he heard my mental question as clearly as the spoken ones.

YES

Morven would later write:

"At this point Paul and Jimahl release the planchette, with Jimahl saying, 'He's gone.' Paul points out more droplets of water on the planchette, which quickly evaporate."

After the Spirit Board session, we reviewed the digital images that Phoenix had taken. There were a series of shots taken with and without a flash in the candle lit room. One of them definitely showed a face – looking very much like a gaunt version of Alex – superimposed over Paul's features. Another photo showed a white beard-like substance projecting from my mouth, covering the chin area. I had a hunch we were looking at ectoplasm and in the days ahead my research into the subject of spiritualism confirmed this.

Ectoplasm, the books explained, was one of the most common symptoms of spirit manifestation. It often forms at the extremities of the medium, fingertips as an example, the substance was described as a lucid pearl-like liquid which evaporates quickly. This had to be the substance we detected on the planchette. The books went on to explain that ectoplasm often appears to exit the mouth of the medium and fan out into the room as the spirit attempts to take physical form.

That evening was a breakthrough in many ways for me. I had somehow received a personal message from Alex. It was subliminal, but it rang through loud and clear. There was a shift in Alex's energy – a new sense of urgency was developing. I understood that what he wanted was simply an opportunity to *speak*. Not just to me or to those of us who had crowded expectantly around the Spirit Board – but on a larger scale to any who would care to listen. Perhaps, just as the procreative impulse in humans eases the fear of death by assuring that we continue to live through our children, Alex too had to be reassured that he would continue to live through *his children.* A King by title on his deathbed, Alex in reality left behind a fractured kingdom.

More questions followed. If he wanted to speak to others, how could this be done? Was there enough time? Where should we go from here?

Morven, forever the most logical of us, stated the obvious:

"Ask Alex."

CHAPTER SEVEN

ASHA AND FINBAR MEET ALEX

The month of February went by quickly and the seasonal tides turned again. This time they brought the first hint of green to the city landscape. I had spent the last several weeks deep in research about mediums. I was intrigued by Alex's statements regarding the use of both a channel and a medium. I had always thought the terms were synonymous. Interestingly enough, I learned that Alex was indeed correct.

Although separate functions by definition, they are undeniably two ends of one thread in psychic operations. The mental picture that came to mind was a typical household current. The electricity itself comes into the home from a utility pole. This raw source of power flows unchecked through the transformer on the pole. The medium is akin to the transformer, pulling in large amounts of psychic current and funneling it through their own body into the room. Left unchecked, this energy can be extremely dangerous to the medium.

The channeler, at the other end of the psychic connection, then becomes the equivalent of a household circuit breaker. The power is received, filtered and redirected in manageable dosages. Using this analogy, I was able to understand the tremendous roles that Paul and I played in our communication with Alex.

To prove or disprove this theory, we experimented with a variety of combinations in the channeler/medium roles. We found that Paul and Phoenix functioned well as a team. Asha and I did not. It seemed as if our talents both leaned toward mediumship. Working as a team, we succeeded in drawing in a dizzying amount of energy, but we found it difficult to control. (Our interesting experience with the Spirit Board is recounted in Chapter 9.)

By teaching me about mediumship, Alex also inadvertently helped me to understand one of the basic principles of Magick. Polarity, often understood in the Craft to represent the balance of gender opposites, is not necessarily dependent upon gender at all. It is relative instead to the successful production of magickal current in exactly the same manner as described in the transformer and circuit breaker analogy.

One person must be magnetic – drawing in the energy. But to utilize the incoming energy productively, another individual must become electrical – channeling the power in measured doses toward the desired goal.

Asha, Finbar, and I were invited to Paul and Phoenix's home for a Spring Equinox ritual. Joining us would be Paul and Phoenix's new students – three unique women whose physical appearance and personalities seemed to embody the three aspects of the Goddess perfectly – Maid, Mother, and Crone.

Since Asha and Finbar had not been present at the previous Spirit Board sessions, Paul happily arranged for them to arrive a few hours before the students to speak with Alex.

We set up the Spirit Board in the ritual room and Paul and I assumed our usual positions. Asha, Finbar and Phoenix sat near by. Since most of this session was private, no notes were taken. I have tried to recreate the most significant dialogue.

Alex came through quickly and greeted us.

5 FOLD KIS   BLESED BE

Asha and Finbar were overwhelmed. Although they had received individual messages from Alex at Lammas, the experience of having a private connection with him was very powerful. Seeking clarification on some difficult personal issues, Asha directed most of the questions to Alex. Aside from the delay factor in having the planchette spell each word, it seemed as if Alex was seated next to us – every response to her complex questions proved to be insightful.

Asha had demonstrated, over the years I had known her, an inherent ability to transcend the physical and literally become a living vessel in which the Goddess could manifest. Although all High Priestesses are trained to perform this function to some degree, Asha consistently delivered far more than most. She gave herself up unselfishly - instinctively tapping into the primal power of the Goddess – and allowed that power to blow into a Magick Circle like a typhoon.

One of my fondest memories of Asha channeling the Goddess occurred about five years ago on a Maine mountaintop.

I had been backpacking with her and Finbar. It was a rough period for me. Faced with pressing personal problems, my life seemed like a worn thread that kept unraveling in the most inconvenient places. We were all much younger at the time – and in retrospect at the height of our physical endurance. Each of us shouldered heavy backpacks as we hiked up a hairline trail to the top of a moderately sized mountain. We started the ascent at mid-day and calculated more than enough time to reach the summit and set up our camp before dark. It would have been a realistic goal except for a streak of darkness that suddenly smeared the horizon – accompanied by the unmistakable rumble of thunder. The storm came upon us quickly with all the usual bells and whistles. We were within a hundred yards of the top – scrambling over boulders the size of houses – our feet resting precariously on ledges barely a foot wide. Miraculously we won the summit without injury and set about putting up our tent. In the downdrafts of the storm, the canvas billowed crazily. Asha took control of the situation, coherently giving instruction to Finbar and me. We were barely successful in getting the tent staked down before the storm unleashed itself full throttle. The three of us huddled in the tent, awed at the unpredictable power of nature. As the thunder broke above my head, I was reminded of a private conversation I had shared with the Goddess the day before.

I had been sitting on the screened-in porch of their summer cottage – feeling very badly for myself. I had whispered to the Goddess – "I've lost my fire. I am depleted. If you are still there for me – I need you to remind me of who you are. *Show me the magick.*"

The storm passed quickly and when we went out into the cool clean air we found that the first stars of the summer evening were already ablaze in the indigo sky. We decided to improvise a ritual. Staring up into the arching canopy of space, both Finbar and myself invoked the Goddess into Asha. For a long while, there was silence. The night thickened and the sounds of the wind moved across the rocky field. And then a voice, small and still, came out of Asha. The voice formed syllables – sounds – nonsensical – and yet each murmur was packed with emotion. Eventually the syllables formed words and the words became a mantra that Asha chanted over and over again into the twilight.

"Sun Moon Stars Planets Spinning Sky Earth Sun Moon Stars Planets Spinning Sky Earth…"

To our delight, Asha was gradually transformed. Her eyes blazed like molten stars and we realized that the Goddess had answered our invocation and now stood before us. Unfortunately, she immediately had a problem with my attitude.

"How dare you tell me to show you the magick," she said. I couldn't breathe, I stared into her eyes and felt suddenly like the most insignificant life form on the planet.

"Everything is magick. Look around you. You are the magick!"

Asha has continued to be a clear vessel for the Goddess throughout the years. She serves the Craft well in that regard.

Unfortunately, whenever the Goddess manifested through Asha, she was not able to benefit from the experience in the same wonderful way as those around her. She decided to ask Alex if there was a remedy to this situation.

"Alex," Asha asked, "When you gave me my message at Lammas it was just one word – *Goddess*."

YES

"Alex, I understand that I have the gift of bringing the Goddess through to Her children. But I also need the touch of the Goddess in my own life. How can I accomplish this?"

I LUV ISIS

It was an unexpected yet appropriate comment from Alex. Asha has always felt an affinity with Isis.

"Thank you Alex. I do too. Isis is a beautiful Goddess."

YES

And then, in response to her questions, he spelled:

INVOKE THN BASK

"Bast?" Asha continued, "I don't understand."

NO BASK

"Bask in the Goddess energy that's been invoked, Alex?" I attempted to clarify.

YES

"I understand Alex," Asha said, "But can other priestesses learn to do this?"

U TEACH THEM

"Alex, do you know our student?" Asha asked. She and Finbar were continuing the occult education of a young lady who had moved out of state shortly after her Alexandrian Second Degree elevation.

NO WOULD LIKE TO

"I would like that Alex. Do you have any advice on her training?"

BRING HER ON ROAD TO THIRD

Asha and Finbar asked another series of complex personal questions and Alex continued to respond articulately. When all of their questions were answered, I turned the subject to other matters.

"Alex, it has been a difficult winter for many of our family. We are trying to follow your directive to keep everyone together and to grow. It hasn't been an easy task. Some of us in particular are facing difficult times. A few members of our family are having a crisis of faith. Do you have any words of advice?"

KEEP HEAD UP KEEP GOING

"Alex, I've been getting the idea lately that there is something more you would like me to do with this information."

YES

"Is it your intention that this information be shared with people outside our immediate Wiccan family?"

YES TELL THEM

"How should I tell them Alex?"

BOOK

"When should this book be written?"

SOON

"Alex, tell them what?"

MAKE MAGIC

The planchette stood suddenly still in the center of the board. Finbar was smiling at me from the sofa. In an occult way, Finbar was perfectly matched with Asha – while she exuded a primal, unapologetic current – akin to the element of water – Finbar's presence always contributed a stable, undeniably ancient energy. As quiet as a stone at times, the power that Finbar generated typified the element of earth – deep, well-anchored and as solid as a dolmen.

"Looks like you're writing a book," he laughed.

I called Morven when I got home later that afternoon to tell her the news.

"It doesn't surprise me," she joked, "Alex has never been afraid of publicity."

My head was spinning. Fortunately, I had planned to take a brief vacation from my mundane job. I would spend that time working on an outline for the project and reviewing all of the written information we had accumulated. One of the first items on my agenda was to tell the others who had been involved in the sessions of my intentions. I was aware that the story I was about to put on paper at Alex's request involved them all. It would not be an easy task to complete without communal support and encouragement. I emailed everyone concerned and waited for their response.

"Like the Fool in the Tarot deck," I wrote, "I have accepted the task that Alex has given me. I am stepping into the void. Although I am terrified, I know this is what Alex wants me to do. I hope that each of you will embrace the project as I have. I would welcome any assistance or suggestions you might have."

Within days most of the votes were cast. There was enthusiasm from all of the expected sources – Morven, Asha, Finbar, Paul, and Phoenix. I felt general acceptance from most of the others. But the greatest resistance to the project came from Willow.

She was trying desperately to come to terms with her friend's death. Lost in her personal grief, Alex was understandably the last thing on her mind. She wished me well, but said she no longer felt enthusiastic about our efforts to communicate with Alex.

"Don't forget you promised him an image of the Goddess," I reminded.

"I won't have time to do that before he reincarnates," she said coldly.

Her ambivalence about Alex had been apparent since All Hallows, and yet her decision not to complete the artwork for Alex puzzled me. I sat on the project for several days, brooding over whether or not I should go forward.

But I had made a commitment to Alex. I believed with all my heart that the spirit of this amazing man was still among us and that all he wanted was one last opportunity to speak. I could not let him down.

CHAPTER EIGHT

PROMISES TO KEEP

On a rainy morning in late March, I have an experience that would dramatically change the scope of this project. I am at the computer in my study, trying to hash out an outline for the book.

The small room is filled with my collection of occult art. Stony faces of gods and angels smile down on me from the walls. A small Goddess altar over the desk holds a an image of Diana, her arms outstretched toward me, and vase of daffodils from Asha's garden. Floor-to-ceiling bookshelves are filled to capacity with jars of herbs, hand-blended oils and incenses.

I had been thinking about Alex intently for several days. It occurs to me that if I place myself in a light trance, perhaps the writing would come easier. At least I could filter out all of the irrelevant thoughts and focus solely on Alex.

I am not the greatest when it comes to trance work so it takes a bit of effort. Eventually though, I am able to alter my breathing enough to encourage a relaxed state of mind. It seemed to be helping immeasurably with my memory recall.

Suddenly I sense Alex very close to me. It is as if he is physically standing behind me. I sense that he wants me to purify myself with salt and water. I push the notion out of my mind and continue writing. I am not in a ritual mind-set and the idea of using water around a computer seems naturally unwise. But the impulse to purify grows stronger. I give into it after a few minutes and go to the kitchen to get a bowl of water and some salt.

Returning to the study, I place the elements on the edge of the Goddess altar and consecrate them with my index finger. I then light a stick of incense. There is a framed photo of Alex on the wall. I take it down and place it next to me on the desk.

I sit down again and try to resume work. Alex's presence is again very strong just behind me. I am dressed casually in my sweats – typical clothing for a day home from the office – but the feeling I get is that my wardrobe is somehow inappropriate.

"Put on a consecrated garment," he seems to be saying. At this point I want to see where all of these preparations are headed so I get up, strip off the sweats and slip into a ritual robe.

"If I have to go through this every time I work on this project," I muse, "It will take years to complete!"

Again, I sit down at the computer keyboard to resume work. Almost immediately, I feel a strange sensation on my back and neck. It is as if some essence of Alex passes effortlessly through me from behind.

My hands are suddenly all over the keyboard. I type rapidly. When I finish a moment or two later I am shaking. I am amazed to read the following. It was typed all in lower case with many misspellings and typos. I edited the text to make it readable.

"I am Alex Sanders, King of the Witches. It has been a long time since I wrote, spoke, moved about in the physical world. Many of you have no doubt forgotten me. Some have not. I would hope that you are in remembrance of me. But I was a man and men die all the time. It is dark here. There is no light. A kind of purgatory, I suppose, if you think of the afterlife as a waiting room of sorts. I could have reincarnated long ago, but I chose to remain earthbound. So I am caught between the worlds. I drift like smoke about you. I inhabit your rooms, your sacred spaces. My spirit goes to the circles where I am welcome. I observe. I watch. I try to teach but it is difficult unless those incarnate are receptive. For who can listen to the words of a spirit, not a man who can stand up and be counted as one to hear, but a spirit of a man once known as King of the Witches. Even now there is rancor among you. There is division. There is doubt that I can exist in this way and in this time. But the irony is that this is the natural order of things. I can do what I wish. I have attained that power in many past lives. I am what I say I am, King of the Witches, and abeyance is due me. If not for any other reason but that I am the forefather of who you are. And as I now am, so you will be and your children's children shall look after you as you look after me. And so the Craft goes on- it never dies. It never stops. It can't - you must see to that. I could care less if you use my name 100 years from now. But the Goddess must have her due worship. I am Alex Sanders, of that there is no doubt. I want to talk about the Goddess. And the Craft of the Goddess - that which is and always has been and that which will continue for ages to come. I want to teach you what I could not teach you in my lifetime. I want to show you the way of all true magick. There is a great circle of life and of being that encompasses all humanity. I can see it from here. We are connected on every level. You often make the mistake in perception to think that your lives begin and end at the end of your own existence. Imagine yourself as the centerpiece of a great wheel. You seem complete in your self. You can turn and move in any direction. You are a circle and your hands, the tips of your fingers, the toes on your feet all touch the perimeter of the circle. But there is so much more. I will leave you now. We'll start again another time. Be in peace and Goddess rest."

I didn't know what to think. I was seriously worried I had just lost my mind. I stare at the words on the computer screen until the screensaver kicks on – this startles me. I laugh nervously and resolve to get some fresh air.

Before powering down, I email Morven and Paul – attaching the message.

"I don't know what to make of this – let me know your thoughts," I write.

Neither of them responds to the email. I am wondering if they figure I've gone into the deep end of the pool and are just being too polite to say anything. *If you can't say anything nice, don't say anything at all*, goes the old adage.

It is three days later and the silence of the others has become unnerving. In retrospect, I understand that the isolation and anxiety I was experiencing was a direct result of a deep empathy I had established with Alex. I had foolishly convinced myself that I was suddenly left alone with this project. I again anguish over Willow's disinterest and worry that I am just imagining the whole thing. The idea that I am making a fool out of myself seemed a real possibility. Nevertheless, my commitment to Alex weighs heavily and I sit down again at the computer to put words to page.

Suddenly, I sense myself entering into a trance deeper than I've ever felt before. It is quite involuntary on my part – I can't seem to stop it from happening - so I just let go.

It feels as if I am floating just outside of my body. Again there is a flurry of activity at the keyboard. It is over in just a few minutes.

When I read what I have typed, I start to cry. I realize, for better or worse, I am married to this project.

"I am Alex Sanders, King of the Witches. I come to you from across the eons. I watch the fire of the sun illuminate a fertile land. I see how difficult it is for those who follow the old ways to see the path that will lead them forward, to recognize the dangers that lie before them. I understand how hard it is for those who love the Goddess to keep a clear mind and unfettered will so that they can be about her business without interference from those who would declaim her virtues and deny even the most basic rights to those who follow her. This is a strange, new world. I find myself inside it as an archetype. I am out of my element. Around me there are faces I do not know and when I seek for those who knew me as a man there is only silence. There is no reply to my inquiry. I am alone and this is a very dry place for me. I will move on soon, as I do not see the need for me to remain earthbound much longer. How quickly they turned to the memory of me but once the time moves by and they forget, then the memory of me fades quickly like a flower. I am forgotten of many, no longer the King of the Witches, and this causes me much consternation.

I see that there is a thread, a river of red life that still flows and it is to this river I am drawn like a moth to the fire. And when I see that there is a circle of elders still following the path I made, I am glad. My spirit rejoices. I understand how important it was to wait until I move on. I see that this has not been in vain. You ask me what I would have you do - I would have you tell the others that magic is real. Witchcraft is real. I devoted my life to it. I saw the age of the Goddess dawn over mankind. I came to the Craft in a time when speaking her name was dangerous. I came to her when the dark of the moon was the only time we could worship her for fear of discovery, when the living room became the temple of Isis and the basement, dark and secret, became the place for our library. How we hungered for our freedom then, how we dreamed of a time when we might utter the secret name of the Goddess in public without consequence. All of this has come about in a short period of time and even now the cult of the Goddess grows. It grows from the dead wood of Christianity, for there are those who see the mother of god as the creatress and wonder aloud why she has been allowed to squander her power in the shadow of a sacrificial son. I see that she is once again in the forefront of a religion that will continue to progress as the years ahead unfold and this is a sign that the way of the Goddess will become more palatable to those who seek her. I see that the ways of magic are no longer hidden and you may find the secrets of the ages on any bookshelf in any store. They are so accessible that the reverse danger is evident – that there is a tendency to take all things for granted, to see them as common things that have no weight. This is a trap of the mind and must be avoided. The mysteries of the Goddess are stronger and deeper than time. They defy time. And I can see that now more than ever they become visible to any one who looks with their eyes. As a path in the forest they beckon and the true seeker has no alternative but to follow. These are amazing times and the keepers of the mysteries must be aware of how critical it is to keep true to the path and to make the way smooth for those who will follow their footsteps. More than ever before man looks for an answer to questions asked for thousands of years. The secrets of space are open to us. The secrets of the earth are open to us. The secrets of the universe are open to us. How then can any true seeker of the Craft be denied? How then can any true witch, or one that calls themselves a hidden child of the Goddess, say there is no magic? For magic is in the word, the spoken word. Magic is in the breath of every child and in the love of the mother for the child - how then can we be sad? How then can we be dismal? Wake up the heart that slumbers and look to the dawn of a new day for it is a glorious dawn. I come to you now as a teacher and entrust you with these words. As fantastic as it seems to you, you must be brave enough to pass them on to any who will listen. You must allow me the opportunity to speak once more before all is changed - before the end of the eon. For there has never been a better time to look at the facts as they are. I devoted my life to the Goddess, but as a man I made many mistakes.

That is the mortal way and unavoidable to the most ingenious of us. I pissed people off to say it bluntly. I turned them against me, particularly at the end when there was no place for me to go but down and it seemed as if they all waited for it outside my door. Like wolves they waited and when the king was dead they wailed like children. How sad I am that I did not have more time, or the knowledge that eluded me all those years. I hungered for a touch of the Goddess and she came to me again and again and still I wanted more. I deserved it, I told myself. She owed it to me.

The Goddess, as we see her, is so small. She is just a piece of our mortal fancies and we envision her in manageable portions. Like a piece of meat upon our plates we cut her up and examine her and when we swallow we want to be certain we don't choke ourselves with her. So she becomes small and insignificant. We dress her and adorn her with memories of past lives and we awaken within ourselves the threads of memory that allow us to see her in a way that does not consume us. But when we awaken any aspect of the true Goddess, we awaken the great beast of the Goddess that has no safety valve attached. We can't deflate her by pulling a cork. She is big, beyond any reasoning - beyond any imagining - and a true invocation of the Goddess takes one into the abyss. We must be prepared to experience all of her - not just the parts of her that we are comfortable with. She is a beautiful Goddess - but she is all that is and was and will be. The earth is the body of the Goddess and the earth moves and shakes and shudders beneath us. The earth can heal and it also destroys - it swallows us whole without apology and begs for more. So the primordial Goddess is more than we can envision and the words of a priest of the Goddess must be chosen carefully for this reason. I honor her. I adore her. And there is no reason for me not to endorse her to you for the way of the Goddess is the path of truth. Go to her then and be absorbed by her - even when she breaks you down you will profit in the end. There are many that profess to know her and who speak the way of magic. Perhaps they read the books and memorize what it is that they feel they should know - but they do not know her. Their lives are devoid of her. They are limited by fears that manage their lives. This fear dictates what they will never become and when it comes time for them to exercise will over matter they cannot do so. They are slaves to matter. Their will is undeveloped, and that is a danger to them. Know then that many are called but few are chosen. Even among your own you can see those that have come to the Goddess untruthfully. They stand on ground that is not solid. Even among your own you must recognize those who are the old souls who have walked this path before. Magic then is serious business. You cannot fool with it without consequence. Mind my words lest you destroy yourself with your own pride. That is the first lesson I would leave you. Be true to your Craft and do not give your word lightly. You must be prepared to back up your word with your life and the Goddess may very well demand such allegiance one day. Why then have I come now to speak this way through you? The answer is simple - you are willing to allow me to move through you. I will use you by your own invitation to say what I will say. And then I will walk away. You ask what it is I want to say and I shall reveal it to you in time. It has been a long while since I had a voice. I must pace myself, and for your safety, I will proceed with caution."

When Morven and Paul receive the second email, the response is immediate.

"Wow," Paul says eloquently.

Morven, although moved by Alex's words, urges me to be cautious.

"Channeling in this way can lack credibility. Traditional methods of divination are much more believable. I don't doubt that this is from Alex. But you are a very intelligent, articulate person and some people may think that the words are coming not from Alex but from your own subconscious. My concern is that if you lose credibility in the reader's eyes, Alex loses credibility as well."

"I understand," I say, "But the end justifies the means. He wants to speak and by comparison the Spirit Board is so laborious. I am feeling a new sense of urgency to gather as much information as possible"

"Stay focused, Jimahl," she encourages, "It will all come together. This is a tremendously important work."

Still feeling shaky about Alex's direct communication with me, I send the messages to Asha. She calls me a few nights later and reads them back to me on the phone. It provides an interesting perspective and it is as if I am hearing Alex's words for the first time. When she finishes, there is a long period of silence.

"I can hear Alex in these words. It is as if he is speaking them aloud."

"I don't know what to do, Asha. Do I include them in the book?"

"How can there be a question?"

"But what will people think?"

"Your ego has no place in this project, Jimahl, none. Remember the promise you made to Alex. You have never broken a promise before. You can't break this one."

"I have to be realistic, Asha. I don't know if I can do this. It's too much."

"Jimahl, you are so fertile right now. You are like a root that has lain dormant in the earth for centuries, and from that root new life stirs. There is fresh growth inching its way toward daylight. If you give up now, the root will die. Nourish the plant, give it light. Once it breaks the surface, the green will keep on growing. Trust me. You have no idea how important it is for you to complete this project."

She ends the conversation shortly afterward and promises to visit in the near future.

"I bought a new Spirit Board," she says. "I'd like to take it for a test drive."

CHAPTER NINE
ASHA AND JIMAHL CONTACT ALEX

Asha, true to her word, stops by for dinner a few nights later. Finbar is delayed at the office and promises to be along shortly. Dave is always happy to see Asha, as they are both artists. This commonality between them has created a special friendship that provides endless opportunities for conversation.

After some lively discussion, Dave excuses himself to work on dinner. Asha suggests we try her new Spirit Board. As an experiment, we join hands over the board before beginning and recite a traditional incantation, making a clockwise stirring motion above the planchette. It seems to raise a lot of energy and when we place our hands on the planchette, we find that it immediately starts to circle the board in a rapid manner. Around and around it goes; our fingertips are barely able to keep up with the momentum.

We both laugh, realizing that the planchette is obviously riding the unseen field of energy raised by our invocation. I remember Alex's words from the last channeling session: "M*agic is in the word, the spoken word.*"

How incredibly clear the art of invocation suddenly becomes to me. Every word we speak has the potential to become a spell, an invocation. If magic is in the word, and if the power of the spoken word creates currents as tangible as this – then the heart and mind of a magician must be forever in control of what is said and thought.

Eventually the movement slows and we are able to gain control of the planchette.

"Alex," Asha intones, "We want to speak with you. I read the words that you gave Jimahl. We are part of that red river you speak of – that thread of life that keeps the Craft alive. Speak to us Alex, King of the Witches."

The response is immediate.

WITH YOU

"Is this Alex Sanders?" she asks.

BLESSED BE

"Alex, this is the first time that Jimahl and I have worked together on the Spirit Board. Is it OK with you that we communicate as a team?"

YES BREVITY

"You're asking us to be brief in our questions?"

YES

"Alex, Jimahl has shared the two messages he received. These are incredible communications."

CHANNELG

"Alex, were you channeling them through Jimahl?"

YES

"Alex, is it better to use the Spirit Board in this way to speak with you? Or do you prefer channeling as a method?"

A N Y

"Any method is fine?"

YES

There is a lull in communication at this point. After a few moments of silence, I ask if Alex is still there. There is no response.

Finbar comes in shortly afterward and we decide to try again. He agrees to take notes.

There is a lot of confusion this time. The planchette moves erratically, first going to *yes* and then *goodbye* – over and over.

"Alex," Asha calls out loudly, "Speak with us again. King of the Witches, answer our call."

The air seems thick with energy. The planchette continues to move in a moronic way. I realize that Asha and I are moving vast amounts of energy but none of it is making any sense.

"We're both mediums," I realize, "We need a channeler to control the influx of astral data. If we keep going at this rate we are going to blow a circuit or two."

"Let's try harder," she insists. "Focus, Jimahl. We can do this."

It is much more difficult than with Paul. My head is throbbing. I feel like a motor on overload. But I finally resolve to allow Asha to draw the energy into the room and resign myself to becoming its conduit. Like two dancers, both trying to lead, I relax the controls, and let Asha sweep me effortlessly across the dance floor.

Eventually the planchette starts to spell real words and a fresh connection with Alex is established.

MAKE MAGIC MAKE MAGIC

The planchette spells the same phrase over and over. There is a sense of immediacy in the message.

"We are the keepers of the mysteries Alex. We *are* making the magick." Asha is now speaking in a trance voice. Waves of energy wash over her and fill the room.

YES BLESSINGS

"Blessings to you as well Alex. What do you have to say to us tonight?" Asha's trance voice was startling. Dave pokes his head in the room and gives me a quizzical look.

BE TRUE TO WORK

"Is this the book you are referring to Alex?" I ask.

YES BE TRUE TO OTHERS

"Do you like what I've done so far?" I was feeling very proud of the fact that I had finally finished Chapter One.

BARE BEGINNING

My heart sank. "Is there anything you can say to help me Alex? This is very difficult."

ASK HPS

"Ask a High Priestess for help?"

MORVEN

"Is there anything else Alex? Any others words of encouragement?" The temperature in the room had climbed. My throat was dry. Finbar was scribbling wildly, a tense look on his face. Asha remained tightly in control of the moment.

PERSEVERE

"I'll try Alex. I'll do my best."

YOU NOW MUST EDUCATE OTHERS

"Will you help me?"

YES BELIEVE

"How much time do we have Alex?" I had a feeling that the stakes were much higher than originally anticipated.

U KNOW

"Alex, I don't sense there is as much time as we originally thought. How much time do we have? Please just answer the question."

EIGHT

"Eight what Alex? Eight months?"

I calculate quickly. It is now April 1999. Eight months will take us into the year 2000. "It must be eight months," I reason.

"Alex," I add, "Is there anything else we need to know?"

There is no response. The energy starts to wane quickly. Asha lets go of the planchette with a great sigh and slumps in her seat. It takes her a moment to come out of the trance. I am trembling, breathing hard, my shirt is soaked with perspiration. I look up at Finbar - still writing feverishly on a pad of paper.

Dave walks into the room carrying a platter of roasted turkey with all the trimmings.

"Alrighty then," he laughs, "I think I need a cigarette after that! Anybody hungry?"

After dinner, Asha volunteers to help me with the dishes. She is standing at the kitchen window admiring a terra-cotta pot of fragrant rosemary.

"Rosemary for remembrance," she says softly.

I think of Willow and silently send her strength.

"Any thoughts on tonight's session?" I ask.

"Be true to the story and the others. But above all, believe." Asha summarizes. "It all makes perfect sense."

"Easy for you to say," I reply, as I toss her a dish towel.

CHAPTER 10

DARK WATER

In the early weeks of April, the thread of communication that we had so diligently guarded starts to unravel. It begins with Asha's curious dream:

She sees herself in a boat – it is night and the water that moves the boat forward is as black as the starless sky. Asha recalls that the boat is old and in need of repair. The dark water seeps in through cracks in the hull. There is an oar missing which makes it impossible to navigate the craft. So Asha resigns herself to the will of the sea. The boat lurches forward on an unseen tide, eventually coming to rest on the shore of a deserted beach. A house can be seen further inland and Asha gets out of the boat and moves toward it. Sounds of friendly conversation can be heard drifting from the house. Asha sees the inhabitants of the brightly-lit rooms through the open windows. It seems as if a celebration is in progress.

Asha is on the porch now. She steps into the warmth of the house. There is a sudden silence – all heads turn in her direction. She is clearly a stranger in this place.

"I'm looking for Alex Sanders", she stammers.

There is a murmur of acknowledgment and someone directs her to the garden in the rear of the house. Asha goes outside into the backyard. The air is thick with flowers, their perfume heavy on the breeze. She finds Alex walking there with a matronly woman on his arm. Asha greets Alex warmly but is surprised to learn that Alex does not know her.

"I'm one of Morven's students, Alex. You've met Morven. Do you remember her?"

Alex again shakes his head negatively. He then extends his hand to Asha and introduces her to the woman at his side, whom he identifies as his mother.

Asha called me the day after the dream and was clearly disturbed.

"It doesn't make sense that he didn't know you," I reassure her, "You just spoke with him last weekend."

As she related the dream to me, I also became concerned. The leaking boat, the seething water, the mysterious house on a lonely island – all of it seemed loaded with dark imagery.

My own dream came a few nights later. Many of the elements were the same:

I am walking at night along the bank of a river. Suddenly a dark wave of water rises out of the river, surges over the bank and sweeps me off my feet. I am thrown into an unrelenting current and am powerless to resist. The momentum of the water carries me forward and leaves me stranded on a strange shore. There is a house in the distance – its windows blaze invitingly. I enter the house, just as Asha did, but in my dream no one turns to acknowledge my presence. I ask about Alex. But no one hears me. I start moving through the festive crowd of people - looking for Alex. They speak to each other fondly –this is obviously a reunion of old friends. But no one seems to notice me. Alex is no where to be found.

'Very interesting," Paul comments when I tell him about the two dreams. "Have you been able to sense Alex around lately?"

"No. I can't make contact with him no matter how hard I try."

"Perhaps we should try the Spirit Board together one more time?"

"Thank you," I say. "If we could speak with Alex again – even briefly – he may be able to tell us what is going on."

We are huddled over the familiar board a few hours later. Paul and I are on the planchette. A link is established quickly but it is very weak. Alex spells out Morven's Third Degree name – it has become a means of identification between us.

Paul and I make a concerted effort to sustain the connection – but there is a definite strain. It seems as if we are playing an astral game of "tug of war" and the other team is pulling harder on the rope than we are. The planchette moves slowly – creeping across the board like the dark water in my dream.

"Alex, can you speak with us today?" I ask hopefully. The response is quick and decisive.

NO

"No? Alex, you've never said 'no' before." I am shocked by his negative response. "Please, Alex, just a few questions…"

There is a moment's hesitation and then:

TRY

"Alex, what is happening on the dreamscape? Can you explain the meaning of these dreams?"

PARANORMAL

"Alex, where are you right now? Why is it so difficult to speak with you?"

SEA OF BLACKNESS

"Alex, there seems to be tremendous opposition to our communication today. "

WOMAN

"Alex, is it a woman who is making it difficult to speak with you? Who is this woman?"

DESOLATION

The planchette creaks to a sudden halt.

"Alex, are you still there? Alex?"

There is nothing. I look at Paul. His face is as long as mine.

"Alex, please talk to us," I insist. "Tell us what to do. Give us some direction on how to proceed. Alex…?"

"It's best to let him go for now." Phoenix says. "He either doesn't want to answer your questions or can't."

"Can't? What's that supposed to mean?"

"I don't know, Jimahl. I don't have any answers."

For a short while we brainstorm about the possibility of potential adversity to the project. It doesn't make sense that anyone would make an intentional occult effort to sabotage our efforts. We go around and around the ring of possibilities until we are exhausted. It seems obvious that we are muddying the water even more in an attempt to see clearly. So we all agree to walk away from it for a few weeks.

Beltane is nearly upon us. The second of Paul and Phoenix's students is scheduled to take her Alexandrian First Degree on May 2nd. They have a lot of preparations to make. I am cognizant of the tremendous amount of physical and mental time this project demands from my friends. And personally, I am exhausted.

"We'll reconvene after Beltane," Paul says encouragingly. "Perhaps we all just need to take a break."

Asha calls with interesting news a few days later.

"I just realized that April 30 will be the eleventh anniversary of Alex's death."

I look at the lunar calendar tacked up next to the phone and smile.

"And there will be a bright full moon that night. I hope Alex enjoys it."

CHAPTER 11

THE FINAL COMMUNICATION

Paul was the one who eventually placed the missing piece into our communal puzzle. On May Eve he had a dream about Alex that pulled the out of focus picture into clearer perspective.

"I saw Alex in Summerland," he tells me excitedly. "It was a huge Beltane celebration. He was very happy – finally he is with other Craft people who have passed on. There are a lot of other witches there. Alex is not lonely any more. He's gone home."

"But what about the dreams Asha and I had?"

"Perhaps the dreams were a premonition that Alex was about to make the transition into Summerland. The dark water in the dreams could have represented the space that divides the world of the living from the world of the dead. There are many multi-cultural references to this void as a body of water – the River Styx for example."

"A sea of blackness?" I interject, remembering Alex's words.

"Exactly, and although rest, renewal and regeneration await the soul after the journey – the trip across that water has got to be scary. Perhaps the woman Alex called 'desolation' is the dark aspect of the Goddess – the watcher between the worlds, the Queen of the Underworld."

"There's still the unsettling fact that Alex did not recognize Asha in her dream."

"I've been thinking about that." Paul says thoughtfully. "You told me at Samhain that you were positive Alex was still earthbound. Do you remember?"

"Yes, his connection with us was so strong."

"This is just hypothetical," Paul explains, "But perhaps when the soul passes over to the other side it sheds the trappings of the mundane self. The sacrifice of remembrance may be a part of that process."

I take a moment and reflect on Paul's conjectures. As much as I want to embrace them, I still find myself resisting the idea that Alex has moved on so quickly.

"He said he would reincarnate in the year 2000," I say stubbornly. "This is only May 1999."

"Jimahl," Paul laughs, "when was the last time you studied biology? The human gestation period is nine months. Do the math. After all, he never said *when* in the year 2000."

I thought about my conversation with Paul for several days. Then one afternoon when I am home alone I feel the familiar rush of energy that I had come to associate with Alex.

It is as if an astral phone is ringing. I sink down effortlessly into a deep trance and a brief flash of communication comes through me. It occurs in the same manner as the previous channeling sessions.

Afterward, I stare at the computer screen for a long while and silently resolve to keep this information from the others.

Perhaps I am playing a psychological game with myself. I believe the message is not only genuine but of tremendous importance. But it also provides closure to these remarkable events. I simply do not want to accept this. I want to believe that the temporary lull in our communication with Alex will end soon. I want to believe that Alex's voice will come again in the greening of the year and that he will continue to enchant and inspire us with his wisdom.

But in my heart I know Paul is right. I remember my joke to Asha about hoping Alex enjoys the Full Moon. Alex *had* enjoyed the Full Moon on the eleventh anniversary of his death. The light of that moon was enough to lead him out of my metaphorical forest and across the dark water that separates the worlds.

I print one copy of Alex's final communication and delete the file from my hard drive.

CHAPTER 12

THE GREEN THAT KEEPS ON GROWING

The first of May turns out to be one of those rare Spring days when it seems as if all of nature is exhaling. Everything smells of blossoming trees and green grass and freshly turned earth. The sky is storybook blue – there is not a cloud in sight.

I have been invited to spend the afternoon at Raven and Jack's covenstead. The windows of the old house are thrown open and the smell of summer awakening fills the rooms.

Sulis and Ruanna are at the table, weaving flowers from Raven's garden into a crown for the Maypole. Their faces are radiant. I look at them – really look at them – and it is as if I am seeing each of them for the very first time. The sun weaves patterns in Ruanna's auburn hair. Her hands work steadily at the crown – each delicate bloom falls from her fingers and is absorbed miraculously into a tapestry of glorious color.

Sulis sings softly as they work – it is an old song, a song of hope renewed and the turning of the wheel from dark to light.

Jack and Morph are in the garden, placing a tall, neatly trimmed, fir tree into a freshly dug hole. Raven runs to meet them. Her long hair is woven with flowers. She ties red and white ribbons to the top of the pole.

The door to the house slams suddenly and Sulis runs down the garden path with the flower crown. Her bare feet make hollow music on the warm earth.

"Wait," she calls out, "This is for the top of the pole. Wait for me!"

Standing at the edge of the garden, I watch as the Maypole is set into place and secured. The wind takes Raven's red and white ribbons and teases them into a tempest.

Morven comes up behind me.

"The Craft is a living thing," she says quietly, "It will never die."

I put my arm around her and pull her closer. "I hope Alex is smiling on us today."

"I'm sure he is," she replies, her face turned toward the white light of the sun. "He must be very proud of all of us."

We dance the Maypole into existence, weaving our ribbons tighter and tighter. As we spin happily around the tall tree, a flash of images rolls across my mind. Each mental photo hangs vividly in the space above our heads. I remember the first time I set foot in a ritual circle, the smell of the incense as it reached me, the warmth of the candles on my skin. I remember Willow standing beside me, watching breathlessly as Morven opened the *Book of Shadows* and began to read the ancient words of power for the first time. I see all of us in the forest – huddling around the campfire as we raise paper cups of wine to the Gods. I taste again every crescent cake ever blessed at circle's end. And I remember in a dizzying, heart-crushing moment every second of elation we felt together, the exhilaration and power of our rituals, and conversely the inevitable moments of confusion and pain when one of us faltered.

'How strong our hearts still beat,' I remind myself, and the ribbons are wound tighter still. 'How alive we are.' And the red and white ribbons at last become a finished work of art, a tangible reminder of how succinctly each of our lives are woven into and around the lives of the others.

When we are finished, a fat rabbit ambles across the green grass. This rabbit seems to be an acceptable omen for our future.

On the second of May I am invited to Paul and Phoenix's covenstead to witness a First Degree Initiation. This is the second of their students to be initiated within the past few months. It is a beautiful ritual, austere in the ways that initiations must be – and yet profoundly moving. At times I feel as if I am floating above the room, watching from a distance. Every gesture, every word, every intonation speaks of ancient magick.

The Craft is alive, as Morven observed. It has survived for centuries despite every attempt to eradicate it. Now I watch breathlessly as the old oaths are taken once more.

As the young priestess takes her solemn pledge, I am reminded again of the enduring power of the Craft.

"I do of my own free will and accord most solemnly swear that I will ever keep secret and never reveal the Secrets of the Art," she says – each word is spoken with unwavering confidence. I can hear the passion for the Craft in her voice.

Three hundred years ago they were hanging witches a few miles from where we stand,
I remember, *And yet here we are - still here – still invoking the most ancient of Names.*
Like the tree that pushes through a tiny crack in the pavement of an urban landscape, determined to reach just a piece of sky, our voices are as strong and resilient as ever.

As the new priestess is welcomed into the coven, I remember the words of a poem I had written in the dark half of the year.

> "Green growing, future knowing.
> Seed of summer sown in spring,
> Conceived by light to rule the darkness,
> Waken to the words I sing.
> By rush of wind, by heart's desire,
> Deep as dark and beyond knowing,
> Be the fire that makes the magick,
> Be the green that keeps on growing."

I embrace the newly-made witch fondly and look into her eyes. I see reflected there the joy of a journey begun.

"You are the new generation," I tell her, "You are the future of the Craft. You must carry it on into the new millennium. You must find the secret children of the Goddess and freely give them what you have been given. A hundred years from now, someone will be standing where you now are – someone will still be singing the ancient song – the Craft will be as alive and vital as it is right now."

I remember something that Morven told me long ago:

"The Goddess will exist only as long as she continues to be invoked. There must always be a keeper of the mysteries. For when the name of the Goddess is forgotten and there is no one left to invoke her – the Craft will cease to exist."

In the impertinent way of a beginner, I did not see the logic in her statement at the time. But now I see clearly that she is right. And the inherent responsibility that accompanies Priesthood is undeniable.

CHAPTER THIRTEEN

AFTER THOUGHTS

As I complete the task with which Alex entrusted me, there are still many unanswered questions that remain. This, I suppose, is understandable considering that the catalyst for the project has been dead for over a decade.

I never did find Fred, who Alex remembered fondly at our first communication. Perhaps I will have an opportunity to speak with him at a later date.

The reason for Alex's decision to remain earth-bound also eludes me. I can only speculate that Alex had a vested interest in making certain that the work he began would continue after his death. Although he had apparently named a successor to the role of *King of the Witches*, this person never stepped forward after Alex's demise. The nature of such a responsibility would inherently include keeping the Alexandrian tradition intact and providing a solid framework for future generations of students. So it is an assumption on my part to wonder if this may have resulted in Alex's last minute decision to stay around for a while and look after his own affairs.

Alex also spoke of a gift that he meant to leave his students at the time of his death. Unfinished business has always seemed the most obvious motive for spirits to remain locked into the space between life and death.

He described this gift in our first encounter as *books*. Perhaps these are most easily understood as physical volumes, similar to a *Book of Shadows*. In a small way, the work you are now holding may be a part of Alex's legacy. But perhaps the books that Alex speaks of are not only those which are bound with paper and glue.

The recurring theme in all of Alex's communications is growth, the preservation of Goddess worship, and the critical importance of working together toward a common goal – to secure and maintain the Craft.

In this larger sense, I tend to envision the *books* of which Alex speaks as the cumulative experiences of us all. The pages of this book become a complex chronicle, a history of many lives – all woven into a magnificent saga that defies logic and spans time. We all contribute to this book whether we realize it or not. Every one of us has a page to write. Each new story is filled with fresh insight and renewed vision. When one page is completed, another is begun. Individually our efforts may seem small and unimportant, but collectively we write a masterpiece – a perpetual story that never ends – because as long as the heart of the Craft beats fiercely, the book of our lives can never truly be finished.

Alex awakened in each of us the slumbering awareness of divine purpose – he reminded us gently that we each have been given a unique gift. In the beginning, our mutual reaction to his attention was much like children around a doting grandparent.

"What about me Alex? Do you have something for me?" And patiently, lovingly, he unfolded each gift in the form of words and gave it over unselfishly.

In retrospect, I realize he also asked each of us for something in return.

My own challenge was simply to listen.

Much of Alex's communication seemed to focus on *togetherness*. When considering the concept of *family* in any context, it is important to realize that each member of a family is a unique and necessary component of the whole. Without the benefit of our individual experiences and talents, the concept of family quickly solidifies into a rigid, inanimate object – incapable of maintaining a pulse.

A spiritual family may be defined as a group of people who share common threads of belief. But a spiritual family is no different than a family in the mundane sense of the word. To say that a spiritual family is defined only by dogma is as ludicrous as saying that a mundane family is composed solely of flesh and bone.

Although the commonality of spiritual beliefs serves inarguably as the framework for a healthy group soul, the real test of a family - *however defined* - is simply how well they care for each other.

I can imagine the Craft as the first bubbling of liquid from an underground stream, the water as sweet and pure as that first tasted by our ancestors. This hidden fountain bubbles up to the surface and forms a pond. It is a deep pond and from the surface it would be easy to dismiss it as stagnant water. But the underground spring feeds the pond well and eventually it trickles over into a small stream. The stream spins lazily through a dry field, giving it new life. On the banks of the stream bloom perennial flowers, fragile to the touch and yet they return year after year in greater bursts of color.
The stream links to a brook, and the brook diverted in a new direction slowly becomes a river. And this river flows to another river and the wide expanse of water follows a silent inevitable path to the sea.

I have been a child in the Craft, standing at that first pond – staring at my reflection in the water and feeling as if I were the only person in the world – disconnected from the whole.

But now, as an adult in the Craft, I accept the responsibility of making certain that no one else will be left staring down into that pool of water, feeling isolated and alone. I will take them by the hand and show them the ocean – as limitless and as boundless as the love of the Goddess.

Like a guardian of a sacred flame, I pass the fire now from my trembling hand to yours.

Be vigilant that the fire never goes out.

This, then, is the challenge I leave with each of you. This is the sacred trust.

We must never fail the Craft. We must never fail each other.

"Keep your head up," as Alex said, "Keep going."

On the morning of the Summer Solstice I finish the first draft of this manuscript. I give it to Dave who reads through it in one sitting. Dave has lived through every moment of the project. He has been a consistent source of encouragement to me.

He finishes reading and puts the manuscript down between us. I am pretending not to notice that he's done. I sit opposite him, staring into a cloudy cup of coffee.

"An amazing story," he finally says, "But I think you have to prepare yourself for the fact that some people may find it hard to believe."

"It is an incredible series of events," I admit. "But if I had made the whole thing up I would have definitely written a better ending."

He laughs and pushes the stack of paper across the table.

"There's just one thing missing," he says. "You never did share Alex's last message."

From my weathered notebook, I take out a folded piece of paper and pass it to him. He reads it aloud:

"You sense me near but are unable to touch, to communicate with me and this frustrates you greatly. I am equally frustrated because I cannot speak to you the way in which you desire. I cannot see you in the way in which you ask me to see you. There are shadows between this world and the next and except in a consecrated circle there is much interference. I hear you. I sense you. But it is difficult for me to speak in return, to touch and to answer your many questions.

The tie that binds us together is the tie of love for each other. I see the Goddess in you and I respond to her. The tie of love that binds us is the love of the Craft that you show forth and I respond to it as I must.

I am Alex Sanders. I am he who you call your forefather. The reason for my presence is clear only to me for it is a path that I have chosen. How long will I remain here? You say there are many who care to listen but in reality there are few who care anymore. There are greater teachers than I to come. I have made a small mark on the face of the cult of the Goddess. I would do more if I could. My time is up and I must go soon into the void, as you would see it. I pass over soon into the heart of the Goddess and from there await rebirth.

I call you now to service. Be strong in purpose and pure in heart. As long as a circle is cast, as long as the name of the Goddess is invoked, she will manifest and grow fat with worship. I cannot say more than that. Never quit. Never stop, for the effort alone carries you forward. Believe in yourself. Believe in the power of your own commitment."

He hands the rumpled sheet of paper to me and stands up.

"Let's go for a walk," he says. "It's a beautiful morning."

"Yes," I smile. "It certainly is."

HAIL AND FAREWELL

EPILOGUE

It has been five months since we last spoke with Alex. The time has gone by quickly, much of it spent in preparing this manuscript for publication. It is exciting to see the *Alex Project* (as my friends have dubbed it) so close to completion.

Although it was never my intention to write an epilogue, I feel compelled to share a dream I had recently. In this dream, I encounter a mysterious woman who seems to function as a sort of astral receptionist. She delivers a written phone message to me. The slip of paper resembles the usual message forms available in most office environments. It reads simply:

Please call Alex Sanders at home this evening to discuss the book. You know the number.

When I remember the dream the following morning, I am both amused and surprised. Amused, because once again Alex's gentle sense of humor comes through clearly. Surprised, because I had assumed after the dark April dreams that he is now beyond our reach.

Although it seems unlikely that I will have an opportunity to conduct additional sessions with the Spirit Board before this book goes to press, I would encourage the reader of this book to be especially sensitive to Alex's presence and to reach out to him by whatever methods possible.

If there is one thing I've learned through this experience, it is that the living tend to dismiss the dead too readily. Perhaps the boundless chasm that we place between the worlds is one of mortal invention. Perhaps communicating with those who have passed through the veil really is as simple as returning a phone call.

So I will end my story by leaving you an open door.

If, while you read this final page, you sense someone standing just behind you, don't be hasty to give your "overactive imagination" all the credit.

In the realm of witchcraft *anything is possible.*

Jimahl

October 1999

ABOUT THE AUTHOR

Jimahl currently resides in Boston with David, his partner of fifteen years.

Jimahl's interest in occult spirituality spans many years. Areas of special interest include herbalism, tarot, ceremonial magick and a strong connection to the folklore and mystery of the sea.

Initiated into the Alexandrian tradition of Wicca eleven years ago, Jimahl considers that experience to be a major turning point in his life. Since then he has devoted his spiritual path to exploring the mysteries of the Goddess and to the preservation of Wicca for future generations.

A Voice in the Forest is his first book.

Jimahl welcomes your comments on
A Voice in the Forest.
Write to him c/o Trident Publications,
P.O. Box 990591, Boston, MA 02199

ABOUT MORVEN
(Preface)

In 1969 Morven stumbled upon a copy of Sybil Leek's *Diary of a Witch*. It didn't take long before she was avidly reading books and magazines on the subject, though it wouldn't be until the mid-70s before she could find much of anything other than astrology and general supernatural in local bookstores. After answering a classified in an alternative newspaper for someone "interested in Wicca" in 1974, Morven attended an Alexandrian ritual and was initiated into a Boston Alexandrian coven in January 1975.

In September 1980, the coven as it existed disbanded and Morven became a solitary. She co-founded *Harvest*, a Neo-Pagan journal, which she led as Managing Editor until the last issue in the Fall of 1992.

In 1988, Morven formed the coven of Na Fineachan Glice, with Jimahl as one of the initial students. The coven family continues to this day, with five covens hived off from Morven's original.

With Alex's prodding, NFG has become more focused these days on "togetherness."

Morven
August 31, 1999

ABOUT THE ARTIST

DAVID TAYLAR DANIELS
(Cover art)

David is a resident of Massachusetts, and has a love for creative expression. His main talent and interest is in the world of art quilting. He has created many beautiful and moving art quilts, each of which speaks with a voice of their own.

It is this use of imagery that has led David to delve into the world of digital artistry. It is his ever-expanding digital portfolio that has allowed him to come up with the cover art, inspired by both nature and the messages from Alex Sanders.

To view his current quilt collection:
http://home.earthlink.net/~davequilts/

ABOUT TRIDENT PUBLICATIONS

Trident Publications is a new company which is devoted to a very simple mission:

To provide an alternative to the major publishing houses for the many writers and artists who have important ideas to share and yet will likely not be published due to the lack of "mass market" appeal in their work.

At Trident Publications, we celebrate the creative impulse, which stems from cultural and spiritual diversity. We hold the integrity of the artist's work in the highest regard.

It is our goal to provide a comprehensive publishing service that provides the tools necessary to bring the artist's inner vision to fruition.

A VOICE IN THE FOREST is our initial project. We believe very strongly in the importance of this book and are proud to present it to you. We anticipate that its success will create a healthy framework upon which we can begin to build our future.

Please tell your friends about Trident Publications and ask for our future publications at your local bookstore.

We appreciate your comments and suggestions. Please write to us at:

Trident Publications
P.O.Box 990591
Boston MA 02199